Room for Good Things to Run Wild

Room for Good Things to Run Wild

HOW ORDINARY PEOPLE BECOME EVERY DAY SAINTS

Josh Nadeau

W Publishing Group

An Imprint of Thomas Nelson

Room for Good Things to Run Wild

Copyright © 2024 Josh Nadeau

All rights reserved. No portion of this book may be reproduced, stored in a retrieval system, or transmitted in any form or by any means—electronic, mechanical, photocopy, recording, scanning, or other—except for brief quotations in critical reviews or articles, without the prior written permission of the publisher.

Published in Nashville, Tennessee, by W Publishing, an imprint of Thomas Nelson.

Published in association with Yates & Yates, www.yates2.com.

Thomas Nelson titles may be purchased in bulk for educational, business, fundraising, or sales promotional use. For information, please email SpecialMarkets@ThomasNelson.com.

Scripture quotation marked CSB are taken from the Christian Standard Bible®. Copyright © 2017 by Holman Bible Publishers. Used by permission. Christian Standard Bible® and CSB® are federally registered trademarks of Holman Bible Publishers.

Unless otherwise noted, Scripture quotations are taken from the New King James Version®. Copyright © 1982 by Thomas Nelson. Used by permission. All rights reserved.

Scripture quotations marked KJV are taken from the King James Version. Public domain.

Any internet addresses, phone numbers, or company or product information printed in this book are offered as a resource and are not intended in any way to be or to imply an endorsement by Thomas Nelson, nor does Thomas Nelson vouch for the existence, content, or services of these sites, phone numbers, companies, or products beyond the life of this book.

Chapter 23's title is drawn from John Steinbeck's *East of Eden* (Penguin Books, 2002) 583, and is not superscripted for stylistic reasons.

ISBN 978-1-4003-4107-8 (audiobook)
ISBN 978-1-4003-4106-1 (ePub)
ISBN 978-1-4003-4104-7 (HC)

Library of Congress Control Number: 2024944750

Printed in the United States of America
24 25 26 27 28 LBC 5 4 3 2 1

To Aislinn,
who was a light
to me
when all other lights
went out

CONTENTS

ACT I: THE ANATOMY OF ANGUISH

CHAPTER 1.	A SYMPHONY OF HITTING ROCK BOTTOM	1
CHAPTER 2.	HYPOCRISY REAPS NO REWARDS	11
CHAPTER 3.	THE WINDS OF FATE BLOW HERE AND THERE	18
CHAPTER 4.	REMOVE THE ORGAN, DEMAND THE FUNCTION	21
CHAPTER 5.	THE MECHANICS OF SAINTHOOD	27
CHAPTER 6.	RELAPSES INTO WONDER	33
CHAPTER 7.	OPEN SELF-SURGERY	41
CHAPTER 8.	STARVED HEARTS	46
CHAPTER 9.	WONDER IS FOOD, NOT FACT	51
CHAPTER 10.	I'LL PRAY FOR YOU	55
CHAPTER 11.	THE DISCARDED BODY	59

ACT II: THE SHAPE OF IMMANENCE

CHAPTER 12.	BRAINS IN A VAT	73
CHAPTER 13.	KNOCKIN' ON HEAVEN'S DOOR	81
CHAPTER 14.	THE LOGISTICS OF LISTENING	84
CHAPTER 15.	TALK IS CHEAP	89
CHAPTER 16.	STRONG IN BROKEN PLACES	95
CHAPTER 17.	DIVINE JUXTAPOSITIONS	101
CHAPTER 18.	KNOWING GOD, KNOWING SELF	109
CHAPTER 19.	A PHENOMENOLOGY OF SAINTHOOD	113

ACT III: THE ARCHITECTURE OF INCARNATION

CHAPTER 20.	FOLLOWING THE HIDDEN MUSIC	125
CHAPTER 21.	THE LONG OBEDIENCE IN THE SAME DIRECTION	130
CHAPTER 22.	THE BLUEPRINT OF A SAINT	137
CHAPTER 23.	"NOW THAT YOU DON'T HAVE TO BE PERFECT, YOU CAN BE GOOD"	142
CHAPTER 24.	THE MYTH OF EXTRAORDINARY	146
CHAPTER 25.	YOU WILL BE FORGOTTEN	152
CHAPTER 26.	BODIES ARE SACRAMENTAL	158
CHAPTER 27.	LITURGIES FOR LOCAL LIVING	164

ACT IV: THE SYMPHONY OF EMBODIMENT

CHAPTER 28.	A STUDY IN DESIRE	179
CHAPTER 29.	LONGINGS FULFILLED	185
CHAPTER 30.	TRUTH IS NOT MERE FACT	190
CHAPTER 31.	RIVERS RUN WITH WINE	194
CHAPTER 32.	ALL THREE, TOGETHER	201
CHAPTER 33.	LIKE BODY, LIKE SOUL	205
CHAPTER 34.	YOU ARE WHAT YOU LOVE	210
CHAPTER 35.	AN ARCHETYPE FOR BEING	217

ACT V: THE MELODY OF NEW BEGINNINGS

| CHAPTER 36. | THE HEAVENLY CADENCE | 229 |
| CHAPTER 37. | CRAFTING A HOLY IMAGINATION | 235 |

CHAPTER 38.	WORKING BACKWARD FROM HEAVEN	241
CHAPTER 39.	SELAH	246
CHAPTER 40.	THERE AND BACK AGAIN	251

Liturgy of the Every Day Saint	264
Acknowledgments	269
Notes	271
About the Author	276

Act I.
The Anatomy of Anguish

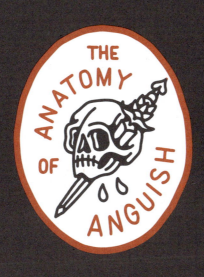

Chapter 1

A Symphony of Hitting Rock Bottom

WHY ARE YOU looking for the living among the dead?"[1]

There's no one here; no one alive, that is. Sure, there's the pretending, the faking, the make-believe, but that's not life, and that's not living. Those are just the death-twitches, postmortem spasms, the continued stiffening of a body drained. It's going through the motions, it's the veneer, the performance. Everything we're *supposed* to do, acting how we're supposed to act. But inside? It's a graveyard.

Stiff and cold.

Lifeless.

It's that space between awake and asleep, that purgatory, where it feels like you're just falling. Where the bottom fell out, everything solid just up in smoke—the same smoke that burns the lungs and stings the eyes. The same smoke that obscures vision, making reality nothing more than a haze. It's the panic, it's the fear, it's the disorientation—no up, no down, just the whistling of everything you ever thought you knew cascading by, as you drop further, and further still.

And then there's the sudden stop.

Like when you shake yourself up from a dream.

A body twitch, jerking awake. Eyes a bit more clear.

And that's what a double of bourbon will do to you at five thirty in the morning.

Rock Bottom, that's what we call it. When you're falling, eventually you hit something: the end, the lowest point. Ground zero. And that's what woke me up—the sudden stop, the bottom of the pit. A moment of depressive clarity.

How did I end up here?

How do any of us end up here? At the Bottom. It's the question we all ask in the haze, in the dream, going through the motions, pretending. It's the question we're forced to ask by whatever shakes us awake.

How?

How did things get so bad? How did things fall apart so quickly? How do I get out? The questions were too massive to answer, at least with my head pounding the way that it was. The only way forward was more of the same. The coping, the enduring, the pretending. The death-twitches. And so, the plan was another one-and-done, a double down the hatch, and off to face another day. A bit of the brown stuff to take all the abrasive edges off my life. Not ideal, but a way to carry on.

I'm leaning on the counter, two ounces of Jim Beam glimmering in my tumbler, all aglow under the pallid stovetop clock, the city's light pollution streaming in from our living room window. The clack and horn of the subway reverberating through our small one-bedroom apartment in downtown Toronto. Newly married to the love of my life, and this was the start to my day. I had been awake for about an hour or so, shuddering at the thought of needing to go another twenty-four hours. The dull throb of my heart pounding in my ears, the sharp pangs of panic in my chest, anger swelling and masquerading as courage.

Just once more.

A lie I tell myself. The lies we always tell ourselves so we can keep on going.

No matter how much you drink, bourbon never goes down easy that early in the morning, and its fire was a wave through my body. This time it was a different kind of sick in my stomach. Not nausea, more like repulsion.

Work was project management at one of the Big Five banks, right at the corner of Yonge and Dundas—Toronto's own knockoff of Times Square. My jacket done up, my bag slung over my shoulder, a salute to my sleeping wife, and it's off into the dreary morning. The city is still mostly asleep, and my bike is locked up behind our apartment. Things felt different, save the numbing that normally accompanies a stiff morning drink. My mind is racing. I'm cycling past cars and street cleaners, my thoughts are on everything and nothing. My hands are cold on the steel handlebars—the rubber taping had pulled away, and so the steel was whatever temperature the cold morning was. Cycling is a rhythm; we all move together in ebbing tides. Rolling past construction workers, past men and women in their office getup. My clothes were a costume. More pretending, more attempts at signs of life. There's the chimes and beeps of streetcar stops and car horns. The sick in my stomach is churning into a storm.

Everything around me was real, but I felt disconnected. In but not of. I felt like a ghost, like half of a person.

So why live at all?

It could all be over.

Everything would be a whole lot easier if it could just end, if I could take that Big Sleep. Stop faking. Get a bit of shut-eye, some damn rest.

Rock Bottom.

It's another lie, but it's one on repeat in my mind: *This only affects me.* No impact on my wife, on my work, on my church. Just me. Collateral damage of zero. I tried to keep up with it all—the demands of life and the self-imposed expectations—but it all demanded *more*. Work was a toxic whirlwind of posturing and politics and partiality, the feeling of never doing enough, of always needing to do more. The nine-to-five grind slowly crept to eight-to-six, and eventually up to seven-to-seven. What started as beers after work with the guys slowly slipped into making sure there was always a bit of *something* to soften me up before heading home, something to cushion the harshness of the day.

The streetlights are a cutting orange against the early morning blue, and the cool air on my face washes away some of the fog in my head. I've made this ride so many times I don't need to think about where I'm going. I know where the streets curve, I know the traffic lights and stop signs, and I know that streetcars can override a traffic light to hold a green, so if you ride behind them, you can catch a few lingering lights.

Legs on the pedals, my mind is just tallying time. That one commodity I didn't have and the one I tried to spend too much of. Maybe all my pain, all the dread I tried to wash away with drink was because I wasn't doing enough. *If I just had a bit more time*, I thought, *maybe I could fix it all*. Marriage had its time costs—they weren't bad, probably the only good thing in my life. But it still cost time.

Work cost the most time, and because of my wife's chronic illness, bringing home the bacon landed squarely on my shoulders. We were involved in a smallish church plant—leading some Bible studies, discipling a few people, and getting some mentorship. More time. It was an easy thing to justify, these demands on my time, because it was for others, their happiness and growth. All it cost was sleep, and a bit of sanity. And so, day after day, week after week, month after month, the slow creep of time consumed me. I slept about four hours a night, trying to lull myself unconscious with some liquor at the end of every day. The days started the same way they ended, and every moment in between was an attempt to squeeze in as much drink as possible. The habit that got me through.

From the outside? Everything in life seemed aces—a perfect little life for a perfect little couple. From the outside it was all smiles and charm, the bright light that everyone wanted to gather around. An up-and-comer at the bank, the poster boy for church vocation, and from all appearances, a pretty damn good husband.

Until I wasn't.

Until the jig was up. Until the storm overwhelmed me. Until the sudden stop. Rock Bottom.

Angry.

Apathetic.

Drunk.

It's a few more streets until work, and the thoughts keep running through my mind, words whispered to myself on my lips. "I'm a mess." Wreckage composed of the collision of apathy and alcohol, the thin veneer of kindness often overpowered by an anger that drove me further and further into drink. A vicious cycle, to be sure. And it's hard to articulate what I felt in that moment—the self-hatred for failing, the wishing some car would swerve and do the deed I was too afraid to commit, the realization that I had been dying for God knows how long.

It was the Bottom. A graveyard.

There is no one here; no one living, that is.

And it was here, as Death appeared before me, that I heard something. Something inside me.

An ache.

A longing.

A song...

THE HIDDEN MUSIC

Some have heard it, that song. It's hidden, a soft and faint melody. And often we're told this music is secret, hard to come by, undisclosed. It's easy to confuse the two—hiddenness and secrecy—but they are different. Secrets are peddled and commoditized. They're marketed to those of us in the pit as answers to all our trials and woes. These secrets are sold to us in all forms of pseudo-spiritual self-help books and seminars. *The Secret to the Good Life. Leave Rock Bottom with Five Easy Steps. Unlock Your Prayer Potential. Triple Your Savings Portfolio. The Body of Your Dreams in a Weekend.* On and on and on. Secrets to save you. All this salesmanship wrapped up with a perfect phraseology to tug at our psychological weaknesses. Finely crafted wordings that hone in on our greatest insecurities, longings, and fears. Prodding in the places that hurt the most.

Am I a good man?

Am I a failure?

Do I have the strength to keep going?

Drink this cure-all, they say. Remedy all the multitudinous pains of life. All for three low payments of your dignity, integrity, and self-respect. Or $99.99, whatever is easier, I guess. Modern-day snake-oil salesmen, preying on the hopelessness and self-doubt of a broken and lost generation.

That is not what I'm talking about—I didn't find magic incantations or some healing potion. There was no secret to save me. The music I heard wasn't like that. And it can't be peddled or sold or manipulated. It is just hidden. Hidden because my ears were calloused; because by all rights, I was deaf.

Give me a moment to explain.

Hiddenness is not a clandestine operation. There's no cloak, there's no dagger; no lurking, no shadows, no marketing ploy. No one is selling you anything. No one is lying to you. Hiddenness is about mystery. Mystery in the sense of mystical. Not the riddles or paradoxes or enigmas of hermits and gurus. Hiding isn't secrecy; it's not even concealing. The music of eternity is hidden for the sake of revealing. That's one of the mysteries of hiddenness—unseen so as to be seen; veiled so as to be revealed. Hiddenness is about the search. The Hidden Music resounds, has resounded, as long as time itself, and longer, whether we have ears to hear it or not.

That's what I heard.

Some echo of eternity.

Cycling through the city with a storm of sick in my stomach, I heard something bigger than all my pain, all my fear, all my anger, all my cowardice. Something was calling to me. Something was begging to be heard, even there at the Bottom. It was alluring, it was inviting. It demanded to be found.

And there lies the Hidden Grace of hitting Rock Bottom.

There's nowhere to go but out or up.

I chose up.

That's why I'm writing all this, everything that follows: to invite you up, and not out. To help you hear what I heard, the still and silent notes of the Hidden Music; to take the first step of the journey into Life, not mere survival. It's not easy, and it'll cost everything, but then, the way I was living was doing the same. Demanding everything yet giving nothing, just dragging me farther down and farther out.

That music I heard, that hiddenness, was my invitation into Reality. More and more of it—an invitation to peel back all the layers of my life and peer into the Truth all around me. In so many ways, I didn't know what Reality was; my reality was a drunken haze, a purgatorial graveyard—the space in between being alive and dead. And this Hidden Music seemed Real in all the ways I wasn't. All the best things in life require an unfolding, a deepening as we commit to them. We're so used to experiencing wonder through novelty that our romance, our religion, our friendships are tainted by some desperate need for freshness. But the best things are wonderful by familiarity; they inspire awe by intimacy. The depth of True Love unfolds before us with each step we take. We never arrive at True Love, we just journey deeper and deeper into it.

That's the call I heard. The call into Infinity. And even there, at the Bottom, it began to set my heart on fire.

That was what I needed, and it's what we all need. Not all of us drink ourselves comatose, but we all have our coping mechanisms, our ways of surviving, and too often we turn to them for salvation. Dealer's choice: porn, drugs, sex, gossip, starving yourself, doomscrolling; it's all the same, and the stakes are always just as high—Death. It's the attempt to numb the pain, hoping that one last hit might take it all away. But it doesn't. It just grows and grows until there's only one thing left to silence it.

And I don't want that for anyone.

VICES, LONGINGS, AND THE WAY TO SALVATION

I lock up my bike in the back alley behind the office, the smell of vomit and regret in the air. Many slept on subway grates to keep warm, surrounded by empty bottles and trash and duffel bags. It was a stark contrast, working downtown; main streets had the big flashing signs, the bright lights, the curated shop windows, all picture-perfect. Yet just around the corner were the broken and battered, the lost and the forgotten. The dirty, the unkempt, the flawed—those pushed to the margins, the outcast. In a lot of ways that was me, that contrast. On the outside, picture-perfect, but look a little longer, and all the broken bits, the battered edges, would come into focus. The same vomit smell on my breath, the air of regret hanging on my shoulders. A whitewashed tomb.

The elevator ride up to my floor was a routine bracing of self. The inhale. The changing frame of mind in preparation. Whatever the questions, whatever the pain, whatever the ache, they would have to wait, like always. The fury of another day's responsibilities would take priority. I walk to my desk, striding under the empty, bureaucratic blinking of fluorescent lights. The ones that sucked all the color from my skin; we looked like phantoms under their glow. At my desk I'm looking out the window over the city. And maybe it was the exhaustion, maybe it was the still-swirling sick of my survival mechanisms, but I knew I couldn't do it. I couldn't fake another day. Not just at work but with myself.

Was *this* the way up?

I couldn't lie about who I was anymore. I wasn't picture-perfect; I wasn't the shined shoes, the tailored pants, the branded button-downs, the hair, the smile. I was broken and battered. I was the back alley.

I sign into my laptop and as emails synchronize, I walk to the break room to get a coffee. I'm washing my mug, rinsing out the dried grinds from the day before, drying with a paper towel, pressing a few buttons on a machine, and watching the burnt rocket fuel slowly stream out eight ounces. And that's the last thing I remember of that day.

It was probably more of the same—the facade, the anger, the drink after work to calm the hurricane. But I do know that was the day everything began to change, mostly because it had to. My vices could no longer be where I went for salvation.

Find life; depart the realm of the dead.

Chapter 2

Hypocrisy Reaps No Rewards

IT'S PROBABLY BEST to lay some groundwork before we go on.

Tales, so they say, are as old as time, and mine started somewhere too. You don't just wake up one day and swap out a well-balanced breakfast for a few ounces of booze. That takes time. And decision. Those two are a powerful combination.

To catch you up, most of my life had been quintessentially humdrum, some outworking of an intense mediocrity. That's how it felt to me: that way down deep, behind all the walls and masks, underneath all the lies and the keeping up of appearances, there was an emptiness. Like I was missing something, like I was incomplete. My life was spent in the church—every time the doors were open, Sundays or midweek, we'd be there—and so, from a young age, the answer to that *missing something* was given to me: God. He was to be the answer to all my feelings of incompletion. That was the story to believe in, the life to act out. Because that's what *everything* is, a story.

My life, so I was told, was to be spent for God, glorifying Him. I didn't know what that meant, but sure as shootin', I'd try. That was the secret potion, right? The cure to my mediocrity? The best Life, so I heard, was the one given to God. It was just a matter of hearing a sermon, reading a book, and doing exactly what you were supposed to do. The best Life, full of Love and Grace and kindness, was just a few commands away. Read the Book, say the prayers, and it would all work out. Count me in—for all of it. All my comings and goings were the attempt at that best Life, dutifully obeying everything I was told and everything I had heard.

And yet it all seemed to come up short. All the effort, all the work, and nothing in me seemed to change. I read the right books, said the right prayers, followed the lists of things to do and things not to do, but I remained the same. Unfinished. Mediocre. Empty. Years of rinsing and repeating yielded only one thing: stagnation, chased down with the inevitable bitterness.

It was the emptiness that haunted me, and there was no keeping it quiet. Inside was this impression that I was made for more, but that *more* was just out of reach. And then there was the terror that my every mistake, my every rebellion, my every divergence from the path would drive me further from my hope: transformation. That's what I was promised: transformation and deliverance. But all that seemed to come my way was guilt and shame for not arriving. There was a way around this guilt—hypocrisy. Pretend. Make-believe transformation. Imaginary Renewal. Bluff my way through it all. Par for the course for me as a way to cover up the humiliation of not finding that life-altering moment. Of remaining un-transfigured.

But hypocrisy reaps no rewards; fake lives have no payoff. There is no freedom in a pretend life, and so, I remained stuck, in between. Half awake, half asleep. Not loving who I was but too afraid to become who I wanted to be. A half a person, kind of thing. But what else was there to do? If God didn't have the answers, no one else would either. So I pressed on, trying the same things over and over, hoping for, expecting, different results.

Enter my vices.

They offered a tangible safety and an immediate salvation. They could be felt. The warmth of whiskey rolling down my throat. The haze and the buzz. Questions melt away. And if the feeling of their immediate salvation ever started to dwindle, I could pour another glass. Vices hear you. They answer you in the way you want: immediately. Unlike prayer, which teaches that you need to wait in order to hear. When life gets hard, when the pains and doubts and questions hit, when those deep and internal conversations erupt in the mind just before going to sleep, it's easy to turn to something to take the edge off. It doesn't matter what you medicate with, we all do it.

I'd be seated around a table with people who I knew did the same thing as me—numbed all the mediocrity, all the insufficiencies of life with something. We'd sit near each other in church, going through the motions, but none of us showed signs of Life. Sure, we learned more, lots of knowledge packed into our heads, but how many changed hearts? How many put the whiskey glass down?

It was the same kinds of conversations, week after week, month after month. People I was mentoring, people in small groups, everyone sharing that they just couldn't seem to make it, to become who they wanted to be, to find that Life we were all promised. Not *life*—like this monotony we were living, this haze of enduring, the in-between—but *Life*, something that could save us. Something that would give color to our drained faces. Something that could wake us up, forever.

Eventually, we all either kept our mouths shut, never telling anyone about our constant struggles, or we settled for pretending and for all kinds of external forms of spiritual maturity. Whitewashed tombs, so the saying goes. That's all we had, the lies, but we all had them together. Misery doesn't love company, it needs it. We need to know we're not alone, even if it's arm in arm on a sinking ship.

It took me a long time to realize it, but everything began to sound the same. Prepackaged, tidied up, boxed, bow on top. No mess. Catchphrases and sloganeering replaced authentic relationships, not because they made sense or because they helped us, but because using the same phrases as some famous Christian, some person who had "made it," proved that we were okay. It was the performance. It didn't feel real; it wasn't *Real*. All of it seemed like a script, everyone reading the lines of a person they were supposed to play. The *Mature Believer*.

Sermons and Bible studies became reruns, or at least copies of copies. That doesn't mean they were all trite and superficial. Some slogans used twelve-dollar words and had the Greek in them, but, at least to me, it was all the same. It felt like the same clutching at acceptance that I was doing. I got through by playing a part, giving enough of an answer so no one would peek at all the brittle bits of my life, poke them hard enough, and have my whole facade come crumbling down. Maybe that's why we all read the script, each in our own way. Because if we saw each other, the real person, we'd all just run away.

Behind those rehearsed lines were real questions that needed expressing, real pain that needed mending; we were languishing, slowly fading; we needed hope, direction, something—but we were all too busy hiding and pretending, too busy rehearsing lines. We wanted love, but we'd never admit it. We needed support, or a shoulder, and if someone asked for it, we tossed a slogan their way, and they'd happily oblige. Back and forth it went: my lines, then yours. It was a performance; it was just what you did. Broken, pretending to be whole.

That's how it all played out, the acting like I was supposed to act, the saying what I was supposed to say, and the insane idea that one day it'd all click. Like magic. Fake it 'til you make it, just at the scale of your soul and eternity. A dangerous gamble. Practice makes perfect, it just depends on what you're practicing and what you're perfecting.

The way of life I had bought into wasn't leading me into the answers I needed; I wasn't becoming Fully Alive—I barely felt human at all.

That way of life didn't answer my biggest questions; it ran from them using fortune-cookie phrases, a prescription of "take two platitudes and call me in the morning." But those won't do when you're wondering if God's real, if any of this makes sense, and why life matters at all.

That way of life didn't teach me about virtue or how to live a good life—it took another shortcut and gave me lists of things to do and not do. The kinds of lists that divided *us* from *them*, the lists that proved our spiritual development. Rules about the approved pastors to listen to, rules about kissing dating goodbye, rules about TV shows and music and clothes and food and drink and words. Opposition to the list was categorized as nothing short of immature rebellion.

That way of life didn't teach me how to comfort a friend whose dad died in a motorcycle accident, about how to support the kid beside me in church whose brother got cancer, about how life is mostly mess and chaos, and it couldn't teach me all the ways Jesus might be present in that suffering. I was, instead, given a six-shooter of banal Christian phrases to blast into my mind every time I got scared. Spiritual suicide.

That way of life showed me nothing of Beauty or how to enjoy Good Gifts, or how all of life—the food, the drink, the sex, the people, the clouds, the sea, all of it—oriented me toward the Source. Instead, I was given the idea that pleasure was the seedbed for rebellion and disobedience and that the majority of life was a joyless trudging. Avoid at all costs, lest you slip all the way down. Lest pleasure lead to bondage.

I was given a burden of guilt with no path to Life.

The entire framework and structure of my living didn't match up with what it meant to *actually* live. It sounded good, and maybe lots of the stuff we told ourselves was "true"—but somehow it didn't translate into growth or change. For some reason, those ideas weren't my instinct when life got hard.

It wasn't the platitudes or dogmas I ran to when Death creeped into my soul—it was the bottom of a bottle.

So how true could it be?

Maybe Truth demands more.

Maybe I wasn't understanding.

And all of that is what hit me. It's what happened with the impact, Rock Bottom, eyes opening and starting to see things as they really were, or at least, what they had become to me. And it was heavy, this awareness that most of my life was in shambles—all covered up with a lie and dolled up to look good. I didn't know how far I'd gone, how much I'd changed. But the fever dream was over; the time in between, the time as half a person, had to come to an end. And it wasn't like I had the answers, it wasn't like I knew where I was going. I just knew where I was, where all my decisions had led me, where all my rebellions and excuses, all my fears and doubts, all my survival mechanisms, spiritual ones included, had brought me—the end. And I didn't want to be there. I didn't want that life, and so, every ounce of pain I felt, every shred of shame and embarrassment, became some kind of calling.

A warning.

And then there was that *Hidden Music*. An echo. An invitation. Some longing for whatever the opposite of this Death I lived out was: hope. My empty life and this heat in my chest, the agony of my current method of operations and the faith that if there was a Bottom, there must be some sort of Summit, these were what drove me.

But before you get the wrong idea, before you think I'm the hero of this story, let me assure you, I'm not.

My mind was a tempest, a storm of apprehension.

Leaving Rock Bottom was one step, but what about the next thousand? What if I failed? Would anyone even understand what I was trying to do? Or would they take all this, all my thoughts and all my flaws, and treat them as betrayal? Would I become a *them*, no longer an *us*? Could I endure the disapproval? And it all threatened to paralyze me. Stuck, there at the Bottom. Were there answers? What would happen when I stumbled, when I needed help? Would I have *anyone* to turn to? Leaving Rock Bottom wasn't a weekend getaway; it was going to take time, and it was going to cost.

Hypocrisy is lethal, hostile to the path of Life.

Chapter 3

The Winds of Fate Blow Here and There

CALL IT PROVIDENCE or coincidence, even fate, it doesn't matter, but I had some help. Throughout high school, I had developed a love for literature and myths, for story. It only deepened in university and throughout my master's. I wanted it all, every tale I could get my hands on. I wanted Wilde and Orwell, Steinbeck and Dostoevsky and Hemingway, Homer and Virgil, Burgess and Huxley. I had read dozens and dozens of stories, and I could see, however faintly, that many of my heroes had gone on some sort of similar journey. Some quest up, not out. Odysseus, Sir Gawain, Robert Jordan—all the same. Confronted with Death and the decision to pursue Life. And these stories became the map of where I was to go; they were all I really had.

The stories were guides, and in them I heard wisdom. I could feel their wind at my back, blowing a bit here and a bit there, helping me forward. I could hear the whispers, the exhortations, and by their stories, I could see where I just might end up. That's what all stories are, or at least what they should be—a way of communicating to us before we can rationally process them, a speaking to our hearts before our minds. Chesterton taught me that—that stories have a freedom to compel us:

> Suppose somebody in a story says "Pluck this flower and a princess will die in a castle beyond the sea," we do not know why something stirs in the subconsciousness, or why what is impossible seems

almost inevitable. Suppose we read "And in the hour when the king extinguished the candle his ships were wrecked far away on the coast of Hebrides." We do not know why the imagination has accepted that image before the reason can reject it; or why such correspondences seem really to correspond to something in the soul.[1]

That the imagination—the heart of my person—could be spoken to through a story, in such a way that moved my soul, captured me when all the slogans and the catchphrases couldn't. That made sense to me, in my core. The corresponding resonance. Story and soul. All the stories I loved were stories that shaped me, and they had sway over me. And in this moment, at the Bottom, they showed me the way. In this moment, they spoke Life and Light into a dark and dying man. Maybe I didn't need all the answers; maybe I just needed some direction.

And that's what I could do, that could be my way up. To be like all my heroes, to follow them, and hear them, and to embrace the same way. In Christendom, we have another word for hero:

Saint.

I didn't know what that meant then, or even what I was hoping for, and I didn't have language for it. But I wanted to understand what it meant to be a Saint the same way I enjoyed a kiss, not by empiricism but by encounter. I wanted to know what it meant to be a Saint by consumption and union. Every part of me was longing to be drowned, but not to Death; drowned to Life, in the Sea of God's Love.

Learn from those who have walked the Path before, they are Guides.

Chapter 4

Remove the Organ, Demand the Function

IT WAS THE night before. The night before Rock Bottom. The night before I crashed into all that needed to change. My wife, Aislinn, is telling me that if things keep going the way they are, if life stays on the same course, we aren't going to make it. It wasn't a threat, it wasn't an ultimatum, it was just the truth. We're sitting on the couch, drinks in hand, looking at each other. We're both in the same room, but we're not *together*. That lie I had told myself, that all my bad decisions only affected me, well, turns out that wasn't true.

Marriages can't last like that. Nothing can. Sure, rings might stay on fingers, but addictions aren't pathways into Life, and using them to survive was just going to stretch everything to the breaking point, waiting for something to eventually give. The slow erosion of love; the death by a thousand cuts. Maybe a year, maybe ten, but eventually it would all tumble down. That was my choice, I guess. "True friends stab you in the front."[1] What my wife said to me that night was a needed knife. It was sharp, and it hurt like hell, but it was the truth I needed. An offering of deliverance. I couldn't hear it then, but it was some of the Hidden Music.

Hindsight is twenty-twenty. That's how we understand our living—not in the moment, not in the present, but by reflection and introspection. By remembering. By contemplation. We understand ourselves, our story, by looking backward. We live in real time, but we apprehend by looking back in time.

Time travelers, are we.

And so, with that compassionate knife plunged deeply into my heart, everything became a moment to assess my living—to try to understand myself, to try to figure out my way forward. Cycling to work, coffee breaks, restless nights after my better half went to sleep—it was all an opportunity to evaluate the *why* and *how* and *what* of this wasteland I found myself in. What was the fertile soil within me in which all this mediocrity was allowed to sprout and flourish?

A few nights later I'm inside a café, late, drinking an espresso, looking out the window, my fingers tapping on my closed notebook. The city is cold, but it's glowing and saturated under a heavy rain; streetlights are reflecting in puddles. The cool of the outside is swelling from the café window.

I'm thinking how there's all these rhythms to my life, all these habits that had oriented me without me even realizing it. But those things, all those habits, they shape us. What you occupy your days with forms who you become. Who knows when drink became my crutch for limping on, but it did. Then it just became a *thing* I did. And that *thing* shaped so much of my thinking and so much of my feeling.

My pen is behind my ear; this couldn't really be written down because I didn't have the words yet. So I just kept watching—cars driving, people walking, reflected doubles of them in every puddle, and I'm wondering if they felt this too. Did they feel the weight? Did they know that every decision, every action, slowly shapes us into the people we become?

It's not just the sermons and the studies that had shaped me; it wasn't just what my leaders said that formed me; it was everything. All of my life. It was here at this café, and it was me at the bar, and me at home with my wife, and me at my desk at work. It was all the times in between, times on subways and in waiting rooms, times walking, watching, and washing. It was every little thing. I was shaped by what

I did, *how* I did, every moment. And if it was true for me, it had to be true for everyone. Watching people now, at work or at church, or even from this café window, was this continual confrontation with the question of where we end up. Where do all our decisions lead us? And what effect do all our little lies have on us? Mine led me to the precipice. Just one more drink. It won't hurt anyone. Unintentionally embracing a way of living that was going to kill me, that would lead me further and further away from who I wanted to be. Everything has consequences.

The café door rings, the bell on the hinge, and a couple walks in, shaking off the cold, smiling and holding hands and ordering something hot, sitting down and staring at each other. Their wet footprints slowly disappearing with every step they take. My journal is open now, and my pen is clicked, and it's tapping on the blank page. Do we all believe the little lies? The ones we tell ourselves and others to keep pretending everything is okay? Will we all offer excuses at the Pearly Gates for why we never took responsibility for who we were and what we did? Do we all let life push us around, maybe even to the brink, and only fight back when we're half off the edge?

Responsibility.

That was it. Ownership. I alone was accountable for the state of my life, and that meant that only I had the accountability to change it. No one else could do it for me. I scrawl out a sentence: *Something is always forming us.* Maybe it's our parents, our pastors, the expectations of cultural icons, but none of them are to blame for who we become. Blame won't do on deathbeds, nor will excuses. At the end of it, we alone are accountable for the life we lead. At the end of it, all that matters is some sort of authentic attempt at the Good. Not passivity.

People are still passing by in the rain, shoulders hunched, collars turned, the world spinning underneath us all. I put on my coat, turn up my collar preparing for the storm. The café door rings as I walk outside and I'm thinking about all the churches and all the people I've ever known and wondering how many of them lived a life that I also wanted to live. It wasn't blame and it wasn't judgment; it was curiosity. It was trying to figure out what it meant to be Good. Not saved but Good. Someone who confronted all the lies and rebellion within themselves, someone who chose to follow even when the whole world around them wouldn't, someone who followed the call of the Hidden Music. Those were the lives I was looking for.

Some people in the churches I went to growing up were as close to Sainthood as anyone could be; they were truly Good people. Not in the sense of being perfect, not sanctimony, but Good because they kept choosing the path toward Goodness when anything else would have been easier. But now my question is *how*. How did they do it? It seemed to me these people had become Saints *despite* the worlds they existed in, despite all the obstacles and all the issues that confronted them. Despite the pretending, the sloganeering, the superficiality. Despite the humdrum of daily jobs, the world around them, and the pressure of church and the world within them. Despite the temptations.

My hands are in my pockets, striding through a crosswalk, and the flashing hand is counting down—12, 11, 10, 9—to a red light. My shoes and socks are wet, and the rain is finding all the exposed bits of wrist and ankle and neck and soaking my skin. The cold gets in deeper. Those people, the Saints from my childhood, maybe they're the ones who didn't settle for the deception, for the sanctimony, for the game. Maybe they didn't sterilize themselves, falsely clean themselves up, for the sake of acceptance and respectability. Maybe they were Saints because they were honest and because instead of covering up, they went in headfirst, looking for real change. For real growth.

There are shining beads of rain on storefront windows, illuminated by the warm glow of the indoors, and they're streaking lines, weaving through other droplets. *I'm a coward*, I'm thinking. *I've let all my fears win*. And as fear settled in my body like leprosy, it had infected and killed so much of what I needed to live well. Like trying to walk without feet, like trying to hold without hands, like trying to kiss without lips. In some desperate attempt to protect myself, I had killed off everything I needed to grow and change. I was making myself weak and naive.

And then I hear it: a whisper, in my mind. Someone I had read before, helping me along the way, helping me put language to my own questions, helping me see clearly:

> In a sort of ghastly simplicity we remove the organ and demand the function. We make men without chests and expect of them virtue and enterprise. We laugh at honour and are shocked to find traitors in our midst. We castrate and bid the geldings be fruitful.[2]

That was C. S. Lewis. And he was right. I had removed the organs and demanded the function. I wanted Sainthood, but I had settled for fear. I wanted change, and Life, but had settled for drunkenness and apathy and anger. It was a self-imprisonment, a tyranny of one.

Fear eviscerates the vital organs necessary for Sainthood.

Chapter 5

The Mechanics of Sainthood

AROUND THIS TIME I got into boxing. I had done some martial arts growing up and knew that boxing would do my soul some good. Some discipline. Some release. No distractions. Just some hard work. My hope was to get my head on straight, to process it all—the drinking, and where and why it started. And then to start mapping out a way forward in ways that didn't hurt my soul, ways that didn't hurt my wife, ways that didn't make me feel less and less alive. I wasn't looking for a workout, and I wasn't looking for something state of the art. I wanted a place where I could disappear, where I could find some solitude from the chaos of my life, where I could let go, where I could just *be*. Space we tend to never make for ourselves, but space we all need. To contemplate. To listen.

A short cycle away from my apartment was a boxing club on the lower east side, a place with some promise. I walk in and the woman behind the desk is lighting a cigarette, slowly making her way out to take her break. Old, heavy leather bags hung from chains on the ceiling; skipping ropes were slung over hooks on the wall; the dumbbells and plates were iron and chipped; and in the center of it all, a ring, ragged ropes, and a bloodstained mat. Wooden stools along the side. You could smell years of training, sour sweat, and the tin smell of blood. I was sold. Here, I could disappear, and here I could try to make sense of it all. I bought my membership and was back for an evening class.

The moment I walked back in the place felt alive, and I could feel a kind of hierarchy. It was easy to see my place—at the bottom. People are warming up, throwing combos on the bags, bobbing and weaving, skipping tricks, and practicing footwork. And there was the temptation to leave, to turn right back around, to not be the guy who sucks in front of everyone. But this wasn't the time for performance, for make-believe living. I knew what I needed, and most of it was on the other side of all my nerves and insecurity; that's the only way to get stronger, to get better. And I'm sure you already see the parallels with my *other* kinds of pretending.

The coaches blow a whistle and we all circle up. One of them is a young guy—tall, sharp, dark hair. His name is Sasha. The other coach is in his seventies and he's wrinkled and stocky, looks pickled; his voice is gravel. The workout starts and it's push-ups and sit-ups and burpees and skipping. We're in two lines, and every whistle is another push-up, and sweat beads on my nose, dropping down on the rubber mat. And slowly everything else in life—all my problems and pains—becomes background. The foreground is the battery acid in my veins. It's all of us, together. Hearts pounding, lungs heaving, arms and legs trembling. Someone yells at one of us on the floor doing the work. Cheers us on. And then we're all yelling, in unison, with every push-up. It's harmonious. A choir of grunting and perspiration. It's so many circuits of skipping and heavy bag work, of burpees and footwork, of sit-ups and planks.

And the whistle blows. We're done.

And we're all hands on each other's shoulders, smiling. Heaving.

The tired triumph.

You know the feeling. When exhaustion gives way to the joy of endurance, when all your hard work pays off. When you prove to yourself that pushing through is worth it, because your body teaches you how strong you can be.

It was months of this. Over and over and over. I had a friend who'd been there for a few years and we decided to spar one night. He told me he would go slow but not hold back. We're facing each other and then he's dancing, slowly, and I can't keep up. He sways and bobs and throws a left hook to the body and I scramble to guard. He follows up, all in the same motion, with a right cross to the face, and all I can do is guard again. This keeps going, his rhythm, the movement—the body, the head, the head, the body—overwhelming me. And then he winks and snaps out a quick jab. Not hard but fast. And it's a split lip. My hands were down.

Other nights were bloody noses. Some nights people got knocked out.

It was how we learned; it was how we got stronger. It was how all the training, all the circuits and footwork and combos, started to make sense. Heavy bags were one thing, but it's something altogether different when the bag hits back. At first, I got tagged every other punch—the gut, the face. But week after week, month after month, punches landed less.

It was a liturgy.

It was teaching my body a new kind of strength and determination. That's how boxers are formed. Those are the mechanics.

We weren't kept safe; we weren't sheltered from pain. We had to get in the ring, over and over and over. We had to have someone clip us when our hands dropped, had to have our coach tell us how our footwork slowed us down, and then have them show us the right way. My coach would work with me session after session because I kept getting caught by a left hook. He'd show me how to pull my right hand back, how to tighten my footwork, and how to counter with a quick jab.

This is the path for all of us, I'm thinking. *It's not just boxing; it's all kinds of things.* It's dancing, it's painting, it's plumbing. It's pregnancy and childbirth. It's fatherhood. It's being a true friend. It's learning that to develop real skill or strength in life, to grow and to change, we need to admit our weaknesses and face them. We need to admit all the things we don't understand, and we learn by commitment and repetition; we learn by doing. We need help in mastery. We can't pretend our weaknesses away. We can't bluff our flaws into stability. We must confront them. We don't need to solve everything, not all at once. Sometimes we can teach our minds with our bodies and sometimes things need to hit back to teach us.

At the end of class I'm sitting on a bench, people are putting jackets and sweaters on top of sweaty shirts, waving to coaches as they head out the door. And I'm realizing: This is how you do it. This is how Saints are made. It wasn't surveillance or slogans that were needed, not some overprotective shelter, and it wasn't pretending. It was the slow and methodical training. It was a continuous rhythm and commitment, a constant sharpening. It was learning to face weaknesses together, in a place where others could help. It was growing. Saints are formed in the fire, in every single brutal and harsh area of life; and they shine in the darkness, but only if we prepare them. I *could* become a Saint, even if I started at the Bottom. Maybe especially then.

I'm watching Sasha take some extra time with one of the other students, showing her the movements for slipping a cross, which is boxing speak for getting your head out of the way of a punch. And I'm thinking again, *Saints are made by making people strong where they're weak, teaching them endurance through embodied practice, so they can run so as to win the prize.* If we want Saints in the real world, we need to take time. Time for ourselves, and time for others. Time to grow, to master, to confront. To find support and mentorship. The strength of the Saint is courage, courage to embrace the burden and walk the path. Courage to face all manner of evil.

The cycle home is uphill, salt in the wound of my exhausted body. The evening is clear, the air is crisp, and I'm comparing my boxing club with so many discipleship programs at church. I'm thinking about the time Sasha took to tighten up my mechanics. I'm thinking about the workout circuits and how they got easier week after week. I'm thinking about how physical it all was. How embodied. I couldn't just read about boxing, I had to do it. And that's the same for all of life. A stark contrast to the mental and intellectual priority of my church life. Discipleship by facts. Maturity through knowledge. *But life isn't theoretical*, I'm thinking. *It's not simply thinking, it's also doing.*

The city swallows you at night. High-rises and skyscrapers line the streets; the dark sky is never punctuated by stars because of the light pollution, and in that, everything felt local and small. The edge of the sky just a few stories above us all. *It was fear that had formed the foundation of so much of who I had become*, I'm thinking. Fear of failure, fear of rejection, fear of never getting it right; fear of being alone, of never finding home, of losing everyone. My tired legs pedal, everything passing by in glowing streaks. Those fears had shaped me, they formed a lens through which I viewed God, myself, my church, my career. It was fear that lay under all my hope for friendship and for romance. It wasn't the trembling kind of fear, not the cowering; it was a passive fear. Too afraid to truly seek out some answers, to admit my weaknesses, to take responsibility for my life. It was like that temptation to turn tail and leave the boxing club because I wasn't good enough. Too afraid of the consequences, and so all that was left was to live someone else's life. Which probably explains all the emptiness and mediocrity.

My hand is on the brakes, slowing to a stop at a red light. Some people are crossing the street in front of me, and they're laughing. *There is something beautiful about the earning*, I'm thinking, *about the process of becoming strong in all the places I was weak.* Green light. I'm coasting now, down a slight hill, and the evening air fills my lungs and blows through my hair. There was something to this *becoming* a Saint. Something empowering. Strength doesn't come free, and it doesn't come in an instant. The strength that marked the Saints was earned every step along the way. Even in the hardest times, even at the Bottom, there was an opportunity to grow.

Things could always be redeemed.

Rigorous embodied practice,
under tutelage, cultivates maturity.

Chapter 6

Relapses into Wonder

THEN THERE WAS the loneliness.

Trying to stop drinking made sleeping harder, and so lots of evenings were spent on walks, alone. Lost in my mind. Wondering if I'd just come unglued, if on my next step I wouldn't be able to touch back down, if I'd fully disconnect from the world I was trying to exist in. Lost in time and space.

There's a boardwalk along the lake near our apartment, wooden planks fraying up, splintered at the edges, a faint earthy scent of cedar, and it all stretches along the shore. It's late—well, early morning, and the lake is as dark as the sky, but I can hear the waves crash against the cement retaining wall. Iron streetlights staccato the walkway, casting their radiance in so many tangerine circles. I light a cigarette. More of this bad habit to replace the other one.

I don't know why I smoked so much back then. I don't know if it was another coping mechanism, a methadone to my alcohol withdrawals. I don't know why I needed it, the cigarettes, as a way to carve out space to think—and maybe I'll never know.

There's this gray space, this in-between, when we're not where we want to be but also no longer where we were. And often, in that gray space, we are dismissed. Judged, even. For not getting Home fast enough. But you know who meets us in the gray space? Who is always ready to meet us? To incarnate? Who is always ready to draw near?

Jesus.

And I think of all the divides—the political, the denominational, the us versus them, the external measurements for maturity—and I think of all the lines they've drawn among us. And then I think, *If Jesus can meet me where I'm at, and if He meets you where you're at, if Jesus can be patient and work on us, bit by bit, maybe we can do the same.*

So it's the inhale. The pause. Cigarette sitting between my fingers. Eyes closed, trying to breathe in peace, but it's just the burning, and then the exhale. Smoke rises, and my eyes follow it up, now seeing the edges of a sea of clouds, rolling, billowing, highlighted by a hidden moon.

No one but me, standing in a shadowed lunar glow.

The waves break and roll in the dark purples of midnight, and you can smell them. Fresh and musky. I'm leaning on the railing, looking out into the dark expanse, and it's all ebbing and flowing before me. Across the lake are flickering lights, whites and reds, and as my eyes keep adjusting, there's all kinds of purples out there in the sky. A kaleidoscope. All warm. All inviting.

And I hear another whisper, another bit of guidance:

The world will never starve for want of wonders; but only for want of wonder.[1]

That is Chesterton again.

Another drag, my cigarette on my lips, elbows on the crossbar, hands clasped, and then the slow release. My breath illuminated by the same hidden moon. This wonder exists whether I see it or not. Tonight it's just me, alone, to behold the wonder.

But too often I'm asleep. And I mean that metaphorically.

Too often I starve myself of this beauty, this wonder, because I'm so lost in my mind, so lost in my fears and my loneliness, so numbed from drink or distraction, that I can't see clearly. That the eyes of my soul haven't adjusted. That it's just dark—no gradients, no warmth, no hidden illumination.

Another way I had removed the organ and demanded the function.

I wanted peace and I wanted Life, but I removed, by a kind of crowding out, my ability to see, to behold, to wonder. The norm was monotony. It was all shades of gray. And then, there were these relapses into wonder. I had it all backward. And it was starving me.

Walking now, slowly, the cork of my boot heels clicking on the cedar planks, my mind is flashing to all kinds of questions of when and how. *When did I lose the spark? When did I settle for living with my eyes closed? When did I become blind to the impulse of wonder?* Is it just what happens to all of us? Do we all just get so busy with school and work and chores and things to accomplish that *wonder* dies? From atrophy? Sometimes, though, life is too big, and it shakes us up, down to our souls, and we can't help but see the beauty. But we're not stirred. We're not inspired. We're just shaken. Rattled. And then it's back to business as usual. Another relapse.

Young me would have considered this a nightmare, and somewhere, between boyhood and manhood, I lost too much. I lost my wonder. My childlikeness. Substituted for rationality and responsibility, for task and tedium. I left too much behind. Somewhere along the line I had begun to settle for explanations of life over experiencing it, begun to understand only by definitions, and not also by adventure.

Chesterton whispered to me again, up from the pages of another book I had read, guiding me:

> The more I considered Christianity, the more I found that while it had established a rule and order, the chief aim of that order was to give room for good things to run wild.[2]

What if I had misunderstood the purpose of my faith? Of the established rule? What if I was all mixed up about the whole order of things? I didn't know what it meant, just then, for good things to run wild, but it reminded me of something. Of being a kid. Of running in a field with my friends, of blue skies, and of a laughter that held the universe together. And maybe I could have that again.

THE CONSEQUENCES OF A BORED WORLD

A few days later I'm waiting for the subway, heading out to meet some friends at a bar on the other side of town, still thinking about my wonderlessness. About how I anesthetize all my pain and grief with alcohol and entertainment and apathy and pleasure. About how I lost too much in my growing up. About my subtle trade from experience to explanation.

People are standing, staggered, behind the yellow line, watching the arrival time on the screen slowly count down. Bells echo through the tunnels and gusts of cold air billow down the stairs as the station's sliding doors open and close. We're all going somewhere, and we're all lost in our own little worlds. The tunnel tracks are black and brown, caked with oil and wheel grease, and there are ads on the far wall for dating apps and medical services.

There's a kid with his mom, and I can hear the patter of his running and the brightness of his laughter over the music in my headphones. Glancing over, seeing his smile, I'm full of the same questions all over again. *Am I simply a product of my world? Modern, scientific, mechanical? Did all my childlike wonder put up no fight?* The train grinds into the station, doors chiming open, and the cold robotic voice over the intercom gives its warning to stand clear of the now closing doors. People are seated, headphones in, bored eyes, looking nowhere, everything quiet. Only the clack and sway and hum of the train in the tunnel. The boy and his mom are on another car.

And if I lost so much, what did I gain? Was the trade worthwhile? Was all this growing up, was all the baggage that came with it, was it helping? Sure, I could explain a lot: the Trinity, ontological arguments for the existence of God, nature-person distinctions. But did I *experience*? Did I thrill? Could I stand, alone, before my Maker and simply marvel? Could I believe in a way that captured my heart?

On these rides I read, and this time it's Lewis's book *An Experiment in Criticism*. The book is old, a tattered red-and-black cover; the wheat-colored pages are dark browns and oranges at their edges. I thumb to the next page, and then, it's that same whisper. That same guidance. The same kind of voice, up and out from the pages in my hand and into my ears and then down into my heart:

> But who in his senses would not keep, if he could, that tireless curiosity, that intensity of imagination, that facility of suspending disbelief, that unspoiled appetite, that readiness to wonder, to pity, and to admire? The process of growing up is to be valued for what we gain, not for what we lose. Not to acquire a taste for the realistic is childish in the bad sense; to have lost the taste for marvels and adventures is no more a matter for congratulation than losing our teeth, our hair, our palate, and finally, our hopes. Why do we hear so much about the defects of immaturity and so little about those of senility?[3]

My answer. There was a way to grow and gain, and not discard. I could keep belief, keep the readiness to wonder; I didn't have to trade it in for sterile dogma. My creed could still be on fire. There were these tempting defects in the process of growing up, and I was living proof of their consequences. But it didn't have to be that way.

Why do you look for the living among the dead?[4] That's on my mind again. And this time it's about bright eyes of wonder. How alive can we be, any of us, if we are not caught up in the beauty of everyday things?

The train rolls on, I'm still reading, and it's about how books should be valued not for *how* they're written but for how often they're reread, by what these books wake up in us. There are lists, Lewis says, of books that have all kinds of technical flourishes, but he doesn't think that *those* books should be admired above the truly great books, the ones that we, the readers, keep coming back to, are beckoned back to.

I lean my head against the window, my eyes closed, and I can feel my chest rise, then fall as I sigh out. That was me, I was that dichotomy embodied. I wanted art and poetry and music and literature; I wanted to understand the world around me, but I had settled for mere explanatory facts about it. Like reading Shakespeare and getting hung up on iambic pentameter rather than the skin-tightening tension of Lady Macbeth trying to scrub out a spot of blood. Like wanting a kiss but stopping halfway to calculate how much faster my heart was racing, how long it took for hairs on my arms to stand on end, to hypothesize about the reality of butterflies in my stomach.

I thought I was living a purposeful life because I could explain it; but that's not purpose, it's narrative, it's description. And it was my tendency to reduce everything to method, to information; to talk *about* things. Growing up, the loss of childlikeness, is about losing the freedom to enjoy something without explaining it, to experience something without needing to justify it. That was the defect that came with age, like Lewis said. We tend to be spectators, either of our own lives, watching behind the glass of explanation, or settling for watching the lives of others. We live through our cultural icons; we watch them live and have some kind of vicarious experience through them. But that's like watching life from behind the glass of a screen—it's not living, at least not fully.

The train makes its interval stops, its repetitive announcements of doors opening on whatever side of the car, and then the next station. People ebb and flow, in and out, doing what we all do, going about their lives. And my mind is on the fact that I have a form of Life but that I deny all its power. My mind is not just on how *wonderless* I am but how wonderless everything else seems to be too.

I knew it by solidarity, that misery that loves company—an apathy and cynicism that was loved and celebrated by the world around me.

How there was a place for a depression of this magnitude. And I also knew by what I saw people reaching for; I knew by the longings. The hunger remains, and we don't all numb it the same way, but we all do try to numb it. We hope there is more than this, more than the boredom and monotony, more than the mechanical explanations. The hope that there is something, anything, that might make us feel or forget that we haven't felt in a long time. It's all the same. Needing a taste of wonder, a brush with the Transcendent. A moment to forget the mundane. Something needed to transform the perpetual grind. The only problem is, we cut off everything in our belief system that might *be* more.

We remove the organ and demand the function.

And then it's my stop.

Do not scorn childlike wonder with mere explanation.

Chapter 7

Open Self-Surgery

I QUIT MY JOB.

It was only a few weeks after that Rock Bottom moment, and it was inevitable. There's no real way to overstate how scared we felt. Rent and bills and groceries don't skip a month because your life is falling apart; and those little lies I had told myself, that my choices wouldn't affect anyone else, well, turns out those break under the pressure too, mostly because lies are not made to last. I felt like Moses and the Israelites leaving Egypt, crossing the Red Sea, and then ending up in the wilderness. Lost. I knew I didn't have the strength to keep going if I stayed at the bank, I knew that all my excuses would win, and I knew that I'd drink myself to Death. So I had to stop. Stop working at the bank so I could stop drinking. But then there was the wilderness.

And quitting a job isn't some secret hack, some magic potion—Save Your Life by Quitting Your Job. I'm not telling you to follow this path, or that this must also be *your* way. Quitting my job was the consequence of my cowardice and bad decisions, my inability to stop drinking while working that job. When we face our cowardice, and when we start to cut out all the coping mechanisms, we must face all the wreckage they've caused in our lives. And my drinking was a burden of my own making. And it affected everyone around me.

We left our apartment and moved in with my old roommates on

the other side of the city; I picked up work as a bike courier, delivering food. We sold off lots of our belongings, put some into storage in my parents' garage, and we carried on in the aftermath of all my transgressions. Scraping by, doing our best, but hoping Life was on the other side.

I'd work six nights a week, and it was best to start just before the dinner rush, around three in the afternoon. Orders would come in on my phone and I'd cruise through the city, picking up pad thai or butter chicken or sushi platters. Order after order, as fast as my legs could carry me. Tonight it's a red curry, and it's going in my delivery bag, and I'm riding to the nice part of town. You buzz in and you have to tell the concierge what room you're delivering to, and he will call up just to make sure the guest really did order a curry. I get the nod and so up I go to the twenty-somethingth floor. While riding the elevator, I take the paper sack that has the red curry out of my delivery bag, take off my hat, try to pat down my hair nice, and put on a smile. Tips are everything for a delivery guy.

The silver doors slide open and down the hall I go, yellow carpets and green walls, sconces in between every unit. A quick knock at the door and a lady opens it with a smile, and I hand her the goods, making a bit of small talk, trying to secure my tip. Trying to pay my rent a few dollars at a time.

"I just started doing this," I say. "I used to be a project manager."

Like she cares.

But I do.

I care that she knows.

I'm just standing there, on the twenty-somethingth floor, handing a bag of curry to some lady I don't know, some lady I'll never see again, needing her to know that I'm not *just* a courier. Needing her to know I can do a lot more than deliver food. The elevator ride back down to the lobby is a pause.

Is this an identity crisis?

Selah.

I hated my job at the bank, and I hated what it did to me, and at the same time it offered me a bit of value, some sort of clout and respectability. Take that bit of identity away and all that was left was the gaping question of my value. The kind of hole you can't fill with lies or excuses.

In between my deliveries I'd cycle up to whatever skyscraper was closest, lean against it while seated on my bike, and read. I'd carry whatever book I could find that fit in my back pocket, and this week it was *Notes from Underground*. A few pages here, a few pages there, waiting for the next hungry person to call me, just enough to chew on while transporting a club sandwich or a Caesar wrap from the downtown core to a high-rise condo some few neighborhoods over.

The Underground Man, the main character of the story, has, by choice, decided on a life outside the norm. He doesn't fit in, he doesn't know who he is, and he doesn't know his place in the world. Partly because he sees the world as broken and partly because he's blind to reality. He has been rejected, and his response was to reject. He was looking for someone, something to blame, and all he has, because of this isolation, is a relentless and oppressive introspection. So he blames everyone else, seeing himself as their better, and raging at them for not accepting how great he is.

And he's a mirror. A bell chimes on my phone, another delivery, and as I pedal, I'm seeing that the book is about me; I'm seeing my own pale reflection in the Underground Man's life:

> Now it is quite clear to me that because of my infinite vanity and the consequent demands I made on myself, I very often looked at myself with frantic dislike, sometimes amounting to disgust, and therefore attributed the same attitude to everybody else.[1]

This is why I drink, I'm thinking. The arrogance of thinking I know better, the demands on myself, and then the frantic dislike, the never measuring up. It's why I needed that lady to know that being a delivery guy was just a momentary lapse in my best life, that I have more value than this. My arrogance is palpable.

In that bike seat, lots of the city passes by underneath my feet—someone's lunch wrappers, the clogging storm drains, the potholes, and cigarette butts. Everything around me is a blur; there are people getting in and out of cars, they're walking from shop to shop, or they're waiting for a streetcar. And I can see myself in all of them. Maybe they feel just as lost and just as rejected as I do, and maybe it's the same in the church. Maybe we're all on the outside, maybe we're all having an identity crisis, all a bit afraid of being found out, of being discovered. And maybe it's for the same reasons as the Underground Man. Maybe it's because we don't, we can't, fit in. Maybe it's because we're broken and too arrogant to admit it.

My bike slows to a stop; I lock it up and head to another condo lobby. It's the same thing—the meeting the concierge, the buzzing, the thumbs-up, and then the elevator ride to their floor. This time it's a young woman; she's smoking and she looks exhausted. Her eyes are flat; she grabs her food, says thanks, and closes the door. And she's just as lost as me, just as tired, just as worn out. The anatomy of anguish.

That's what I felt. Being unable to participate in the Fullness of the world around me. How many of us are here, on the fringe? On the outside? Maybe it was my arrogance that drove me to the periphery, the thinking that I knew better. But out there, on the edge, it's lonely. And it's tiring. And, oh God, I just want to go Home.

Arrogance chokes growth before it can begin.

Chapter 8

Starved Hearts

WHEN YOU SLOW down from the pace of a multibillion-dollar bank, everything else seems to stand still. And in that stillness, a whole slew of new complications emerge—because something needs to fill the void. It only takes a moment for your problems to catch up to you; and all it takes is knocking down one vice before another wants to come and take its place. And underneath those vices are what drives them.

The passions, the desires, the cravings.

That's what I was trying to numb, what I was trying to kill off—the feelings that drove me to my raging discontent. *Stop feeling altogether*, I thought, *just cut it off at the source. Embrace apathy. I can't hurt if I can't feel.*

There were a few spots in the city that offered a bit of solace, great places to go and think, to enjoy something analogous to peace and quiet. There were rooftops, benches under bridges, and tonight, it is one of the courtyards near the Bay Street banking buildings. It is easier to relax in the evening, the cool enclosure of nightfall. The noise of the city, the constant murmuring of cars and sirens, of horns and people, of everything, carved out a place to simply *be*. Like the boxing gym. Everything and everyone is so loud and so busy and so distracted that not a single person paid me any mind. It was these paradoxical moments where life could get sorted out, where I could try to make order out of chaos, make sense of my embarrassment, my shame, my questions, my doubts.

It was the routine: a cigar up and out from my jacket's breast pocket, and that bought me about forty-five minutes to an hour of peace, of not needing to feel the pain, of using just enough of my body and mind to keep focused on thinking. A little liturgy.

I lit the cigar, inhaled, and tried to remember a time when life was simple. The old black and white. Idealistic. Utopian, even. When everything made sense, where everything had its place. Exhale. There would be no going back to times like that; for now it was this feeling of detachment, the discontent, and tired eyes. The thin, dancing line of smoke trails up from the cigar in my hand, and I'm just as aimless and lost. Here today, gone tomorrow. Inhale. *How do I fix this? How can I make up for all my mistakes? Is this journey, this attempt to leave Rock Bottom, worth it?* Exhale. I can feel the temptation to apathy swell in me, and I know exactly what it is because I've felt it so many times. It's a calloused unwavering. It's the denial of self, but not the Good kind. *Maybe,* I'm thinking as I inhale, *that is my solution. Stop feeling. I don't need wonder if I don't crave anything.* Exhale.

And then there's another whisper; there's this thought, not my own but in my head:

The sickness is always the same, it's just the symptoms that change.

It's Steinbeck, calling out from *The Winter of Our Discontent*. And he goes on to talk about how a character is envious in her poverty and snobbish in her wealth—"Money does not change the sickness, only the symptoms."[1] And her sickness is my sickness. It's the discontent and it's how much virtue we are willing to give up to satisfy our cravings. It's the realization that I was tempted to shift the symptoms. I wasn't solving anything. I was trading drunkenness for apathy. A shell game for my vices.

My take, now, on this side of it all, is that we think we need to kill the passions at the source. *We can't be discontent,* we think, *if we can't feel anything, if we don't want anything.* But the passions, the desires of the heart, they don't kill easily, and they don't go down without a fight. And often, they pretend to be dead, but they live on as a kind of apathy or a duplicitous purity.

Apathy is throwing the baby out with the bathwater; it destroys that which makes us human—a free and loving heart. In the attempt to find contentment, to *be* content, we destroy the very mechanisms that will get us there—we remove the organ. Desires are always signposts, they're notes that hum along to the Hidden Music. Desire is not the enemy. Hunger is not an evil, it just depends on what we satisfy our appetites with.

And starvation is not an option.

The duplicitous purity is the hypocritical lie that everything is okay, that we have no issues, no addictions, are slaves to nothing; and it's a veneer that's about as brittle as they come. Poke at that veneer long enough and eventually everything collapses. We can only keep up appearances for so long, and in the rubble lie all sorts of our hidden rebellions, the remnants of enslavement.

Both were true of me.

The apathy and the veneer. Slowly chipping away at my humanity, playing the part of husband, church leader, friend, insert-anything-here, yet decaying in discontent on the inside.

Descending into some Shadow Realm.

People are walking by, down a short set of stone stairs, making their way back to Bay Street. Out of this tucked-away place. Little clouds of cooled breath puffing up around their heads, glowing a bit under the streetlights. And as my cigar smolders, burns to the very end, I stomp it out and join them. Out of the tucked-away place, a place where I could sit and listen, and back into the noise and flow of a busy city. There is no standing still. We all go all the way, either into apathy and hypocrisy or into wonder and Truth. There are no half measures; every choice affects us, almost completely.

And I know now what I didn't know then: that I was restless. That I had become "to myself a wasteland."[2] That every choice made, whatever way I was trying to find contentment, was leading me further and further into a kind of barrenness, enslaved to nothingness. I thought that becoming *less* human was the answer, and look where it got me.

"Restless is our heart," Augustine said, "until it comes to rest in thee."[3] I was looking for rest, looking for a lasting satisfaction, something bigger than all the temporal fixes, bigger than the transitory numbing. I thought the answer was less, but I was wrong. It needed to be the Transcendent, the Eternal, the Unchanging.

But all I had was that pain in my chest, that unfulfilled longing, and the question: Can any of it be rescued?

Desires are signposts that lead to rest.

Chapter 9

Wonder Is Food, Not Fact

MOST OF LIFE is a circling back, the second attempt at figuring things out. And wonder is one of those things that takes a few tries to understand. That's because we don't lose wonder in an instant, and it doesn't come back just as quick. Wonder is a living thing, and it feeds on belief. It is nourished on faith. And wonder isn't alone in its *aliveness*; love is the same. Love isn't a fact, it's a food. And love doesn't stand still. We're always growing in love, either closer and closer or further and further. There's no neutral ground; no-man's-land doesn't exist when it comes to love. My wonder didn't simply disappear.

I starved it to Death.

But maybe the opposite could be true.

There were rooftops I would go to in the city and one of them was my neighbor's place. We were living with my old roommates above a restaurant, and from the back patio it was easy to climb onto the roof of our second floor and jump over to the adjacent roof. From there, even only a few stories up, you could see the whole downtown skyline. On cloudless nights you could see the glowing aura of the city reaching up and out into the night. I spent a lot of time up there. You could also sit on the edge of the shingled roof, and some nights all of us, my wife and my roommates, would sit up there in a line, having a drink, telling stories, and looking out over our city. Thinking how it could all just fit in your hand, and then the day after, you'd be swallowed by it.

It was a fresh way of seeing the city, of understanding. Sometimes, in order to understand something in its details, in its up close, we have to step back, take it all in. See the forest so we can understand the trees. That rooftop was my own stepping back, and it wasn't just from the city, it was from most of my life. I'm sitting out there, by myself, watching the lights of cars pass by on the street below me, watching the still and vivid skyline, stark against twilight's haze. My life was like that—I was too close to it all, it was too near for me to understand. To see the big picture. I was lost in the weeds, stuck in all the minuscule details. I needed to take a step back.

All the details of my life, of all our lives, tend to obscure and steal focus. I was lost in all these swirling questions of identity and value, of boredom and addiction, of doubts and fears and shame, of not knowing what every next step should be. And all these thoughts haunted me, every moment, lurking around every street corner, in every pub or café, even on my couch or in my bed. But maybe if I just took a step back.

The word for all my feelings, my wonderlessness, was *disenchantment*.

I had bought into a way of living—a naturalistic, scientistic, machine world with a bit of Jesus sprinkled on top. My world, my way of life, my entire way of being had been demythologized, un-magicked. I reduced everything to method and explanation, and that way of living starved the wonder out of me.

But maybe the opposite could be true.

Maybe there was wonder everywhere. What if all of it, every day, was a liturgy? What if I just needed eyes to see? I had removed the organ and demanded the function, but I was learning I could feed it again. And what if everything was food? How I woke up, how I had breakfast, my attitude doing chores, delivering takeout all over the city. What if all of that was a kind of *food* that fed Love and wonder?

While looking out over the city, over the noise, I hear it again, and I'm almost expecting it. The still, small voice, deep inside me:

> For what you see and hear depends a good deal on where you are standing: it also depends on what sort of person you are.[1]

What I saw and heard in this busy world were cogs and wires and machinery. What I heard was the whir and grind, the chug of steam and combustion. The machine. That was my perception; it was the only way to see when your eyes are scaled. But what if those scales dropped? What would the world look like then?

There's another voice:

> Yet our culture takes pride in disproving and exploding the sources of enchantment, explaining away one mystery after another.... We have yet to learn we can't survive without enchantment and that the loss of it is killing us.[2]

It was my deafness and my blindness that was killing me, unable to hear the Hidden Music, unable to see the magic of every day life. I had divorced every bit of Supernaturalism from its Source and explained it away with some kind of counterfeit. It was a spirituality without the Spirit, a living without a pulse, a feasting without a tongue. But there was a way to be re-enchanted, and it was through *the food* of Love and Wonder. It needed to be experienced, and I needed an entirely new way of being alive.

Souls are reenchanted through the food of Love and Wonder.

Chapter 10

I'll Pray for You

TIME ISN'T A constant, at least not in all the ways we think it is. It had only been a couple of months since that drunken morning, my moment of depressive clarity, but it somehow felt like a lifetime ago. The days felt so slow, and I seemed to be making so little progress. I didn't have anyone to tell me that growth comes gradually, that revelation can't be rushed for all the same reasons oak trees can't be rushed. Time. They start as seeds, and then they bloom. All I felt was that I wasn't doing enough.

Have you ever felt like you were coming apart at the seams? Like your whole self is beginning to unravel? Like if someone were to pull that stray thread, you'd come apart? With every bit of me that was undone I felt the temptations to go back to my old life—to medicate, to survive, the same old ways. And truth be told, lots of times I did. Lots of times I didn't know what else do to, and lots of times I just gave in. A few ounces to ease the pain. The path up, not out, following the Hidden Music, well, it turns out it's more winding than I expected, and it turns out it's easy to wander.

It's about eight in the evening and I'm locking up my bike, walking to the Bishop and Belcher, a pub where I'm meeting one of my friends, a leader in the church we were attending. We're seated on the patio, under some red awnings; the amber glow of globe lights and the late autumn air are sharp on my hands and in my nose. The waitress comes, and we both order a pint.

Our drinks come and we cheers, and then there's this moment of silence, and the inevitable:

"I'm worried for you, man."

My shoulders shrug. "Why?" I ask.

"It's how much you're drinking," he starts. And the cliché of the situation isn't lost on me, as I drink a beer, trying to survive this conversation. But I am wondering how he found out.

He sighs. "And you haven't been at prayer meeting in a long time."

And he sort of catches himself, like he's about to say something more, but then thinks better of it or gets stuck on the words.

My fingers are turning my pint glass in its place, the beading condensation turning the paper coaster underneath it to pulp. "Go ahead"—I nod at him—"Say what you need to say."

"Don't you think the two go hand in hand?" he asks, but it sounds more like telling, not questioning. "That if you prayed more, you'd drink less?"

"I'm doing the best I can—" I start, hoping to share some of what's been going on in my life, but before I can, he's back in.

"It's not working, is it?"

And I felt that: like my best wasn't enough, that my best was too late. I mean, he wasn't the one drunk at five thirty in the morning, so maybe his way *was* better.

"I just don't think you're doing your best," he says, cutting the silence. "That's why you haven't been showing up to church and study and prayer meeting. That's why you're drunk and why you had to quit your job, and why your wife has to suffer through it all."

"You don't know how much I'm trying," I say. And I'm on defense. "How much I pray or read my Bible, how much I want all this to stop."

And in my mind I'm thinking, *You don't really care either.* But I don't say it, not out of fear but out of the awareness that the sentiment won't land, that it would just make all this harder. I'm thinking, *He didn't ask how much I pray, or give, or read; he just sees the outside, the mess of me trying to figure it all out, and that's all the proof he needs.*

"You know drunkenness is a sin, right?" Another question that's more preaching than inquiring.

"Yeah," I say. "I know."

There's another pause, and we're both crossing our arms and zipping our jackets farther up, trying to stay warm, each leaving tons of thoughts unsaid.

The back-and-forth goes on for the rest of our respective pints, weaponized catchphrases for all my manifold issues. Then I'm draining my pint glass and he's telling me that the joy of the Lord is my strength, that I need to acknowledge God in all my ways; he's diagnosing all my spiritual deficiencies. I can see all the ways he's right. My problems are no small issue. But the diagnosis didn't seem to help.

We're looking at each other now, wordless. The patio tables are huddled around stainless-steel propane heaters, and there's the hum and smell of gas in the air. He's sipping at his beer. And I just keep thinking how easy all this would have been if I'd never started the journey up at all. If I'd just kept all my problems to myself. If I'd just kept faking it. Sure, it would've hurt like hell, but at least *this* wouldn't have happened. The lie is easier to live, in some sense, until it kills you.

This was part of my path upward.

"Maybe you're right," I say. And it's harder to get out than I imagined. "I don't really know anymore. Life isn't going the way I thought it would, but for whatever reason, I can't seem to fix it. And for whatever reason, everything you're saying never fixed it either."

And there's not much to say to that, I guess. The unstoppable force of his way of fixing life meeting the immovable object of my not giving in. The agreeing to disagree.

We finish the night trying to make jokes now that the heavy stuff is out of the way. I pay the bill and we're both putting on backpacks, walking out to the street, him off to the subway, and me off to my bike.

"I'll pray for you," he says.

Salt in the wound.

"Thanks," I say. Polite. And we wave goodbye.

It is a gift that life doesn't go as planned.

Chapter 11

The Discarded Body

IS HE RIGHT?

My reflection is passing by in so many car windows beside me, all of us, their cars and my bike, rolling through a quiet and slow city evening.

Am I still not doing enough?

Is that the way to think about all of this?

Something about that conversation didn't feel right, even though it sounded true on the surface. I had done all the checklist things, the to-do lists, for so much of my life, and still, when things got hard, I went to a drink. Not prayer, not worship, and not peace. Something wasn't making sense. Turning down a side street, riding past old houses with trees planted in each front yard. Most of them bought and split into three apartments—a basement, a first floor, and then the top floor. There's speed bumps on the road to make sure no one uses it as a shortcut, speeding through a small residential area to skip traffic. One hand is on the handlebars, the other one is hanging at my side.

And there's a memory, a vignette of my life, on replay in my mind.

It was from my seminary days, doing my master's. It was the beginning of the second semester, in my third year, in the evening, and I was sitting in the graduate students' study section of the library. It was just some desks with dividers on the far side sitting underneath the stained-glass, tiled windows. The vanilla smell of old books in the air. One of my classmates was sitting at the desk beside me, both of us writing a paper on Moses' song in Exodus 15. It was around seven in the evening and I heard, "Are you hungry?"

Music to my ears.

An excuse to get up out of Hebrew and into a different kind of brew.

I answered, "Yeah, what do you want to eat?"

He reponded, "Oh, I'm feasting on this passage."

Not a joke.

No embellishment.

This really happened.

He asked me if I was hungry just so he could tell me he was already full. Not with actual food but with food, secret food, food someone like me knew nothing of. He had the ability to be nourished off the meat of the passage, while lesser folk like me required the carbs, fats, and proteins of a burger. The ole bait and switch.

I didn't know how to answer.

"Okay," I said.

And then I left, off to find edible tribute for my hungry body.

And with that memory, with that awkward conversation from a few minutes ago, something clicked as I cycled, as I put two and two together.

All of these people think that there's something spiritual, if that's the right word, that surpasses everything that's physical. That the soul and all the activities of the soul are what we should focus on, to the almost complete neglect of the body. It was a thread that pulled all the way back to my feelings of mediocrity and every apparent solution given: Tend to your soul. It was a reducing, a dividing, of the entire person to nothing more than spiritual, implying that the body is bad, the soul is what matters. And that's what shaped most of my life—a disembodied view of Christianity. A man cut in half, soul carved out from body. A corpse and a ghost.

I'm taking the steps up to my unit, the wooden door with the number two painted on it, the doorknob cold from the entryway. My way of trying to fix my life had been to only do soul stuff. It wasn't about feeding my body or disciplining it; it was about feeding my soul, making sure my soul was on the right path. My journey, I'm thinking as I unlace my leather boots and hang my jacket, was only a spiritual one. And all the ways that I had indulged my body, I was taught to believe, would lead nowhere but down.

Aislinn is on the phone, so we wink at each other as she heads to our bedroom to chat, and I'm opening the fridge, grabbing a Tupperware of some leftovers. This is a kind of Gnosticism, I'm thinking, believing that the body is bad and the soul is good. I place a pan on the steel spiral burner and turn the heater dial; and I'm thinking that even though not many in my church world would call themselves Gnostics; even though we wouldn't say the material world is evil, that our bodies are kinds of prisons, and that some secret, spiritual knowledge will save us; even though we'd all probably condemn that as a heresy, we still live like Gnostics, functionally. Like my seminary friend who didn't need real food, like my friend at the pub who recited scriptures like they were incantations, like me, who drank myself comatose because if my body was bad, why care about it at all?

The leftovers are in the pan, sizzling; the stove fan whirs, spinning the steam up, and it's starting to make sense to me why the spiritual to-do list wasn't cutting it. Why there was nothing to sink my teeth into. I put the leftovers into a bowl, turn off the heating element, and sit on the couch, eating. There is no substitute for nourishing the body; we all have to eat. We can't neglect it. But I had neglected my body in so many other ways—like neglecting a garden, like neglecting a bad habit, like neglecting a spouse. There are all kinds of complications that grow in the shadow of neglect.

Aislinn walks out of the bedroom. "How was your night?"

"What I expected," I tell her. "More of the same—being told I'm not doing enough praying or reading, and if I just did more, then I'd be fixed."

"I'm sorry," she says.

"What can you do?" I say. "But I think I get it now."

Aislinn just nods, encouraging me to share.

"He sees life as primarily spiritual, not physical," I say. "So did I, at least up until about half an hour ago. Something clicked because of that conversation. I realized that I'm living as half a person. Like I'm disembodied."

"What do you mean?" Aislinn asks.

"I mean that I've been treating everything as spiritual. That I've been neglecting half of who I am, the muscle and blood and skin and bones. All of my living has been separated from the fact that I'm a real, physical person. Embodied."

There's a pause.

"My church life," I continue, "my friendships, even our marriage—like some wool of spirituality was pulled over my eyes. Like I had to do it all—my whole life—without my body. Like my body was just along for the ride, but like a husk to carry my soul around."

Aislinn nods again, and she says she feels that too, the treating everything as spiritual. "It's like every book or sermon or bit of advice we get from someone is saying we're just a few steps away from the life we want. But no matter how much we do, how much we follow the rules, we don't get there. We can't take the steps," she pauses for a moment, "because we're not using our legs."

"Yeah," I say. "You're right. And if our bodies are just means to some spiritual end, with no real inherent value, it's so easy to abuse them."

She has a mug of tea in her hands, and she puts the saturated bag on a coaster on our table, then says, "The consequences of all our bad choices don't seem to matter if we don't care about our bodies. As long as, even for a moment, we feel good. Right? You could poison yourself with bourbon night after night, with no real regard for your body, as long as it numbed the pain."

"Because that's all that mattered," and I'm nodding, agreeing. "Some sort of relief, not even thinking about the collateral damage."

Every once in a while you can hear the laughter from people in the restaurant below; these pauses in our conversation, they're what happens when something hits you in the soul.

"I'm filling the void with drinking, but think of all the ways everyone around us tries to fill the void. Food, porn, social media, gossip, being so busy they never have to think—it's all the same thing: poison."

"It feels good," Aislinn says, like it's hitting her too, "to have a bit of reprieve from the pain. But it never lasts."

"It can't. We can't save our souls while neglecting our bodies. All that does is split us in half."

We talk for a bit longer, but it's getting late, so I kiss Aislinn as she heads to sleep. Most of the lights in the apartment are off, save the stovetop lamp. There's some light pollution streaming in from the living room window, glow from restaurant signs and streetlamps, cutting rectangular beams across the walls. Where the body goes, so goes the soul. And when I would use a few ounces to take the edge off, to feel some release, to forget, it wasn't just poisoning my body; it was poisoning my soul.

And then there's another vignette playing in my mind, from my time back in seminary.

I was being mentored by one of my profs. We'd meet, week after week, in his office on the second floor of the small, white seminary building. Some of what framed our conversations was a book by R. Kent Hughes, *Disciplines of a Godly Man*.

"This all feels empty," I say to him. "Not us meeting but the book and the questions I'm supposed to ask because of it. Like it's saying the right things, but it's not getting in me. I'm not changing."

He's leaning back in his chair, elbows on the armrests, fingers interlaced, the clink and chime of the white water radiator hissing in the corner. He had one of those doorframe pull-up bars in the corner of his office, and there were some dumbbells there too. "Lots of these guys," he starts, "just think their bodies are useful for carrying their souls and brains around."

And I can tell he's not saying anything in particular about R. Kent Hughes but about a way of being, a way of existing.

"Is that why, even with all this information in my head, so much of it feels hollow?" I ask.

The seminary was on a busy street corner, and from his office you could hear the construction workers on the street, and there was a draft blowing in from the wooden window frame. He pauses for a moment.

"Many scholars interact with the world in a cerebral matter," he says. "And if there's a blind spot, it's that they don't use their bodies in their work, and so when they write their books, the blind spot remains. Not all of them, but some. It's an intellectual Christian walk. A disembodied faith."

"And so when they write these books about our Christian walk," I say, "it sort of follows suit. Spiritual, intellectual, and not physical?"

"It's why the same few answers are given in every area of life," he says. "It's why when we have lots of talk about discipleship or formation, everything gets reduced to a handful of intellectual spiritual practices. Fix your marriage, your parenting, your job, anything, with another sermon or study, with a bit more prayer, Bible reading, and tithing."

I just nod. But it doesn't all make sense. At least it didn't then. But, as the memory fades and I'm back, sitting in my apartment living room, it starts to come together. The facts of my Christianity were only part of the whole. Religion is a practice, and Truth is part of that, but it's not all of it. Embodiment is the whole. Engaging the whole person. Most people were just like me, tending to only their souls, but neglecting their bodies. And that's why, I'm realizing, we feel disconnected, why we feel half-alive. Like looking for the living among the dead.

I head to the bathroom to brush my teeth and try to wind down for bed. I'm staring at myself, brushing, in the mirror's reflection. And I can see it, the halfness of it all. It's why my eyes seem dull and dead. It's why the spark is gone. I spit out the toothpaste and wash it down the drain.

Then there's the other side of this, the idea that if the body is bad, anything of the body must be bad—cravings and desires. All of them. I'm waiting for the water to warm up, and I'm lathering some soap, washing my face. The desires for sex and for food and for everything in between—they are treated like they're some kind of deficiency. Reaching for a towel, rubbing my face dry, I'm thinking that if those desires, those hungers, are bad, then the way to tend the soul must be through denial, always. That's what I'd been practicing—the denial of every kind of pleasure. Cure the disease by killing the patient. Remove the organ.

I hang the towel back up, flick off the bathroom light, and head back into the living room to grab my empty bowl of leftovers. Maybe it's easier to think denial is the answer than it is to have some kind of proper teaching of the body. Of how to value myself as an embodied man, and the desires for sex and satisfaction. Maybe it's easier to use shame and guilt as weapons aimed right at all my desires, as a way to move me to a kind of obedience.

The bowl goes into the dishwasher, same with the spatula, and then the pan goes into the sink; I turn on the faucet, waiting for the water to heat up. Leaning with my back against the counter, I realize that's where all my pretending had come from. It was because I was settling for something other than Fullness, pretending that living as a half person, as just soul, was enough.

But it wasn't.

I'm scrubbing the pan, the water running over my hands, droplets splashing on the countertop. I needed to feel alive. To feel the blood in my veins again. I just didn't know how. My person was divided in two, and all the king's horses and all the king's men couldn't put me back together again.

And then there's another whisper, another guiding voice:

A man is not a man without his body, just as he is not a man without his soul. A corpse is not a man; but also a ghost is not a man.[1]

It's Chesterton again, and he's making all kinds of sense. I thought I was being *more* spiritual—the body neglected, the soul treasured. Instead I had become a specter, a ghost in a shell, disembodied, and because of that, there was no way to genuinely participate in the world around me.

I head to the bedroom, still stuck. I don't know how to put myself back together, to wed my body and soul. I didn't know then that our bodies were made to reveal, to make the divine tangible, to sing the Hidden Music to everyone around us. I hadn't read what John Paul II wrote:

> The body, in fact, and only the body, is capable of making visible what is invisible: the spiritual and the divine. It has been created to transfer into the visible reality of the world the mystery hidden from eternity in God, and thus to be a sign of it.[2]

All I knew that night, lying in bed, was that somehow I had bastardized my body, cut it off from its high calling and used it as a way to conceal. Conceal all my pains and insufficiencies and brokenness. But try as I might to hide all my sins and secrets, my body bore the scars of all my rebellion; unveiling all my own hidden mysteries, because that's what it was made to do.

Souls cannot be restored
while bodies are neglected.

A LITURGY OF ANGUISH

Find Life; depart the realm of the dead.
Hypocrisy is lethal, hostile to the path of Life.
Learn from those who have walked the Path before,
   they are Guides.
Fear eviscerates the vital organs necessary for Sainthood.
Rigorous embodied practice, under tutelage,
    cultivates maturity.
Do not scorn childlike wonder with mere explanation.
Arrogance chokes growth before it can begin.
Desires are signposts that lead to rest.
Souls are reenchanted through the food of
    Love and Wonder.
It is a gift that Life doesn't go as planned.
Souls cannot be restored while bodies are neglected.

Act II.
The Shape of Immanence

Chapter 12

Brains in a Vat

IT WAS SAFE to say that my life was in shambles, a "one step forward, two steps back" kind of thing. I started going to therapy.

There were some personal questions to be figured out, ones that were a bit more than I could handle on my own. Trying to map out why it was that, when things got hard, I got drunk. This wasn't the dream. My plan wasn't to mess up the first year of marriage by emptying as many bottles of bourbon as I could, by quitting a secure job, by moving my better half into a spare bedroom above a restaurant and having her share a bathroom with three guys. But as far as I could tell, this way was my only way up. Every other decision felt like a slow descent back to the Bottom.

It's easy, you know, to go back—to survive the way we always have. That's why they say "old habits die hard," because we feed them, forever. We go back to all the coping mechanisms because it's all we have. The devil we know, and all that. Sure, life for me was a hell, but at least it was a hell I understood the rules for. Solomon said, "As a dog returns to his own vomit, so a fool repeats his folly,"[1] and that was how I had spent my life—the perpetual returning.

But I couldn't do that, not anymore. If I did, it'd be the end of everything I loved, whether all at once or a slow Death over a lifetime. And that was a price I was no longer willing to pay. So I took those old habits out behind the shed and pulled the trigger twice. Hoping this time, they'd stay down.

I'm riding on the subway to my next counseling session, recalling everything Raymond, my therapist, had been talking about the week before; mind churning over questions about thought patterns and upbringing and times when I felt hurt or broken or betrayed. Him asking all kinds of things to suss out the feelings behind and under so many of my actions. He wanted to see and understand. And as I'm processing it all, Bob Dylan is singing and strumming in my headphones, telling me there's some Shelter from the Storm.[2]

We'd spent the last session mapping out my responses, the ways I reacted to the things that scared me or hurt me, probably as some attempt to figure out *why*, why did I react certain ways? My elbows are on my knees and my body is swaying to the tempo of the train. His questions had been about my survival skills. Was I an escapist? A victim? The grin-and-bear-it type? Would I shrug it off with a joke? Would there be the attempt to numb the pain with distraction? With entertainment or work or pleasure? And I told him that I didn't know.

I didn't know because I couldn't think of a time when I'd *felt hurt*. But that sounded like another lie to myself. It wasn't that my heart had never been broken, not like my soul had never been crushed, and even though I had cried only a handful of times, I wasn't immune to agony and anguish. The bleeding heart was not celebrated in my circles and so I'd kept it all locked away.

Leaning back in my subway seat, I started to see another way I'd removed the organ and demanded the function, another mechanical way of living. Feeling was a weakness, never taught explicitly, but it was easy to read between the lines. It was the impassive and indomitable spirit that garnered adulation. But Raymond had thrown me for a loop. His questions seemed to crawl into every nook and cranny of my heart, soul, mind, and body. They seemed to expose the lie that I *could* stop feeling. They shed light on the idea that everything I was doing was *because* of feelings, even if I didn't want to admit it.

The subway car grinds to a halt, voice over the intercom mumbling some directions, and the doors chime open. I walk off and head to exit up the stairs. Tiled walls read College Station, slow people shuffling to the right side of the staircase, those in a rush scurrying two steps at a time on the left. Dylan is still singing in my headphones, but it sounds less like him and more like Ecclesiastes:

> "Vanity of vanities, all *is* vanity."
> What profit has a man from all his labor
> In which he toils under the sun?[3]

And I was just exhausted. From all this toiling, all this labor, all this trying to be whole on my own. All of life felt like some wearying duty, and that indomitable spirit—that didn't come cheap. It was not a bargain deal. And Raymond had exposed all that, exposed the toll all this toil was taking on me.

Then there was this weight.

Heaviness on my shoulders, in my chest, and some pangs in my eyes. A pulse and throb in my body. I'm still walking up the stairs, trying to think through why I feel so damn tired. Why does my entire person feel fatigued? My heartbeat is reverberating in my ears. My legs feel fragile. My hands tremble.

I'm just surviving.

No matter what happens in my life, I try to shoulder it. I try to bear any burden. To withstand any storm. Even if it costs me myself. I had this thought that I needed to give myself for the sake of others. It's my duty, my responsibility, my calling. And maybe that's why I repressed all the *feeling*—I didn't have the time. Feeling would just slow me down, a distraction from all I thought I needed to do. And maybe that's why I was so damn tired.

> The sun also rises, and the sun goes down,
> And hastens to the place where it arose. . . .

> All the rivers run into the sea,
> Yet the sea *is* not full;
> To the place from which the rivers come,
> There they return again.[4]

And round and round it all goes, the same kinds of days, over and over and over, and then we die. The same grinning, the same bearing, the same collapsing into bed, not going to sleep, just shutting down. And maybe, because of it all, I couldn't feel anything. Starved.

> Then I looked on all the works that my hands
>   had done
> And on the labor in which I had toiled;
> And indeed all *was* vanity and grasping for
>   the wind.
> *There was* no profit under the sun.[5]

And I began to weep.

Stepping up out of the subway tunnels, off the tiled staircase, into a stormy city, tears pouring down my cheeks, rain bouncing off my hood and shoulders and backpack. My breathing was heavy, feeling like I could wail; like I wanted to howl; like I wanted to run or explode or disappear. I didn't know. I just kept heaving and walking and pushing through the crowded streets to my appointment. I buzzed into the building, took the elevator up, walked into the office, waved at Carol the secretary, sat down, head in hands, and cried.

Just cried.

That waiting room will forever be, to me, a sacred space. A sanctuary. There were no bronze bells, no stained glass, no ornate altar. But it was there I began to let go. I was becoming undone. My feelings, my body, had slipped past all my defenses, teaching me.

"Josh?"

Raymond was calling me into his office, and in his voice I heard something of the Hidden Music—faint melodies of kindness and care.

His hand is on my shoulder as I walk in and sit down on his couch. The irony is that a few sessions ago, when I first started seeing him, I'd yelled at him halfway through our first session for trying to fix me or tell me he knew better.

"That's not why I'm here," I told him. I knew best.

And now, so many weeks later, I'm crying, realizing how exhausted I am, how cold, how detached, waiting for someone to give me shelter from the storm.

"Raymond," I say as my crying stops, as he just sits there, waiting. "I feel severed from life, like everything is a dream of a dream, like the blood is drained out from me."

Raymond has his clipboard on his lap, and he's looking at me over his glasses, his legs crossed, and he's nodding.

"I feel anemic," I say to him. " I feel like I've been running myself ragged, wandering, searching for God knows what, and if I keep going, drifting, I'm going to walk off the edge of the earth."

And then I'm crying again. As though a decade of emotion is crashing upon me like a wave.

And Raymond isn't telling me anything, he just asks, "Is that where the strength comes from? The charm? The knowledge?"

He sees all the ways I have been coping, the ways I used to hide who I really am.

"I don't know," I say. "It's just how I get through. And I guess it isn't working. It's wreaked all manner of havoc on me. Especially thinking I know it all or could explain it all."

And Raymond does again what he does so well: He nods.

And I keep going. "Like I'm a living embodiment of the idea that I'm just a mind, mostly brain and rationality."

"I know what you believe," Raymond says, and he's talking about my Christianity. "How has that impacted all of this?"

"It was just another thing to know and master." I'm sitting there, thinking and processing everything. "And I knew it all. I was catechized growing up—the creeds and confessions, systematic theologies. I'd be in Sunday school, at eight years old, going through the parable of the fishes and loaves with my church friends, and Monday through Friday I'd be working through Berkhof's 'The Knowability of God' for family devotions."

He nods again.

"From a young age, it just seemed like I had most things figured out." I pause for a moment. "I mean, my faith is supposed to be the answer for everything, and I've got a master's in it, but then you wake up and you're drinking before work in the morning, you feel like you're alone, and you weep through the city, and now I don't think I know anything at all."

We sit there for a moment, and Raymond is patient.

"I don't even know if God loves me," I say. And then I'm dumping again. "Sure, I could tell you about God's Love. I know the theology. His Love is unconditional, it's everlasting, it's incomprehensible, it's supernatural, and it's transforming. I read the books, I know the passages. I write papers and sermons and lessons on it. I understand it intellectually, rationally. I have all the definitions, all the descriptions, all the answers. But I never really, truly experienced it. Felt it in my bones. The fire in my soul. The kind of Love that changes a person. The kind of Love that pumps blood into a weary heart. The kind of Love that gives the heart wings and beckons it to soar the skies. My relationship with God is primarily intellectual, cerebral. 'Gray matter' kind of stuff. But a burning heart? Falling in Love? Feeling *loved*? I don't understand that at all."

And we pause again. I look out the translucent window, and I can hear the pitter-patter of raindrops. A drumming of creation.

"Jesus loves me, this I know, for the Bible tells me so," I say. "But I don't just want to *know* Jesus loves me—I want to feel it."

"That's it, Josh," he says. "You want to *feel* loved."

Leaving his office, back out into a misty city, more questions on my plate. *When one thing gets pulled, tugged at,* I'm thinking as I descend back into the subway tunnels, *the whole house comes toppling down.* And then the all-too-familiar whisper, almost expected these days, the voices who will not let me think only my thoughts. This time it's Lewis:

> God has not been trying an experiment on my faith or love in order to find out their quality. He knew it already. It was I who didn't. In this trial He makes us occupy the dock, the witness box, and the bench all at once. He always knew that my temple was a house of cards. His only way of making me realize the fact was to knock it down.[6]

That it was all going to come toppling down, that was the plan. I'd thought I was safe and secure, but my whole life was fragile, brittle, built up on every frail bit of strength I had. And it was a Grace, Lewis is saying to me, that God knocked it down. Because the rains come, and the winds, and there is a Real Shelter from the storm.

Faith demands renovation;
Grace demolishes that which will not sustain.

Chapter 13

Knockin' on Heaven's Door

I'M LYING IN bed, wide awake, just like before, except instead of the haunting loneliness creeping in at the corners of my thinking, it's the wondering if life makes sense at all. Wondering if any part of me understood Christianity. If I had even been in the club to begin with.

The greatest commandment, Jesus said, is to "Love the LORD your God with all your heart, with all your soul, and with all your mind,"[1] but I didn't understand the verb of the sentence. The loving. That feeling of love, the tangible expression of *being* loved, was lost on me. Love requires a vulnerability that was easy for me to forfeit in the name of "success." And success can be anything, really. The cost of love, that vulnerability, had been too much for me to pay.

Beside me I can see the rise and fall of my sleeping wife's chest. Lying on my back, eyes constantly adjusting to the dark bedroom, I'm wondering about all the time spent trying to earn love. I was hiding. I thought love was earned by hiding the real me and presenting, performing, for everyone else. It was the charm and nonchalance and the vanity of all my knowing. I hid behind duty and obligation, a pseudo–messiah complex. And it was easy—because people loved those things. All it meant was that everyone close to me didn't *actually* know me. All they knew was the curated me I put up on the stage, the one I fabricated, the me I felt comfortable showing. And that's what we all do, isn't it?

And it's exhausting.

We think love needs to be earned. Whether it's in the pub or the pew, it doesn't matter; it's still transactional. Product self, curated and polished, up on display, and everyone pays you with their love. The real you, however, never feels it. Because they aren't loving *you*, just like they weren't loving me. Because the real person was hidden. Disguised. The fake me got all the hugs and the smiles; the real me, buried away and exhausted, says: "Jesus, show me Your love." That was the asking, the seeking, the knocking on heaven's door. And I needed it to be opened. And then the real me falls asleep.

There's all sorts of things I wish I could have told myself then, as I stared at the ceiling, wondering if the prayers would be answered, wondering how it was all going to shake down. I wish I could have told myself that prayers are always answered and the path up, out of the pit, is always worth it. That the walls need to come down. I know the pain, I have the scars, and I know the fear. But there is hope. There is a coming dawn, a time when things will start to make sense again, when light will shine on the path. There is a real Love, and it's worth giving everything for because it will consume you—heart, soul, mind, and body. And it will call you up out of yourself, up out of the small and the pretend, and into Fullness.

Into hope.

Into Life.

Divine Love is not earned,
it is a Gift freely given through prayer.

Chapter 14

The Logistics of Listening

WE HAD STARTED going to a new church, and in the late winter the women went away for a retreat, something my better half was a bit reticent about. Caution, for so many reasons, was the name of the game. A few assurances that it would be all right, that she'd have a good time, and things were settled. The Friday came, her ride arrived, and she was off to a cabin in the woods. I turned on some Bob Dylan, got out my tools, and set out on a few jobs for the apartment. The rest of that night was washed down with a book and some black coffee.

Saturday night my phone is buzzing and lighting up, vibrating and ringing, Aislinn's smiling face on the screen, and I'm excited to hear her singsong voice.

"I need to come home, now."

She's in that space between anger and crying.

"What's going on?" I ask.

She tells me it's been horrible. That for the last two hours she was berated for her illness. That all her questions, her doubts, and yes, all her genuine physical pain, happened to her because she didn't *know* the right stuff, because she didn't *believe* it enough. Ais goes on, telling me that they kept reciting verses *at* her, like incantations, her telling them she knows the verses, has prayed them, and is still in pain. She says that they were upset that she had questions about how

God could be good and loving when she experienced so much pain every day, and not just her but so many other people who suffer so deeply. She says they tried to force her to repeat prayers while at the same time looking at her with those all-too-familiar judging eyes. She says that it felt like an interrogation and a trial—the jury finding her guilty.

She hangs up, texts me after, saying the pastor's wife came in, gave her a hug, and said that she was so sorry for what happened. She was out for a walk during the Inquisition of Aislinn. Another text:

I'm coming home in the morning with the pastor's wife.

Sunday morning dawns and Ais is at the apartment door early. We go to our bed, and she weeps. Like the dam that held back years and years of pain and questions and doubts and fury and judgment was obliterated. I'm holding her, and I have no words. And we lie there until it's done.

Then we're in the kitchen having a coffee, talking it all out, and there's a phone call. I answer and it's the pastor's wife apologizing for what happened, for the foolishness of it all.

"It almost seems par for the course," I say to her. "Like the only way we know how to help people is to beat them to Death with the Truth. Like the only way we know how to change someone is intellectual."

She apologizes again, and we hang up.

Aislinn and I sit, holding hands, at the table.

"That's not how it works, you know," I say to Aislinn. "We don't fix ourselves by only thinking the right things."

"I know," she says. "But it still hurts to be hit by it, to be made to feel like all your issues are your fault, and to be attacked, over and over, with things you've already thought, things you already know, until you either succumb or leave."

"I'm glad you left," I say. "I lived that lie, and look what it did to me—almost erased me into nothing at all."

Steam dances up from our coffees.

"It makes you wonder," Aislinn says, "if they're doing all that—the reciting—not just because they think it's the only way, but because if they stopped, even for a moment, they'd realize it wasn't."

I'd known drunkenness was wrong, but knowing it didn't stop me from downing a double or two too many. People are addicted to porn knowing that lust is immoral, knowing that chastity, or the virtue of purity, should be pursued. The same goes for our gluttonous and indulgent culture: We know we shouldn't be mastered by our appetites, but how few of us put down the extra slice in the desire for temperance? We know that hoarding—the greedy accumulating and storing up of treasures on earth—is called a *faux pas* by Jesus, but that doesn't make us generous; we're often greedy little cheapskates, cutting corners at work, stealing and defrauding all for our own benefit. We know that laziness is a corruption and a shrugging off of responsibility, and yet, that knowing will not bestow on us the virtue of diligence and persistence. We're familiar with the notion that envy and covetousness are shortcomings, that being jealous of someone else's car or spouse or job or looks or anything is a deficiency, and still we persist. The same goes for every other vice: anger or pride or lying or gossiping. We understand that these things are sin, but that simple intellectual hat-tip will not change our lives. Knowing isn't enough.

James said, "Even the demons believe."[1] But that belief, that knowing, doesn't stop them from all manner of dark workings. When we reduce all of our knowing to mere thinking, we disturb the balance of who we truly are as humans.

But why?

I kept meeting with Raymond even after my moment of truth. And that proved harder than I could imagine. It was hard to look at someone, be with someone, who had seen me so weak, so exposed. But I took the gamble and showed him the rest of my hand. I told him how hard it was to come back and darken his doorstep after my frenzy. He nodded in his patient way.

"I don't know why, Raymond," I said, "but I wasn't going to come today. Or ever again."

Then the pregnant pause of him nodding and listening and waiting for me to continue, which I couldn't help myself from doing.

"It wasn't about running. Or hiding. I've done that my whole life. This feels different. Like a kind of damage control—"

"What do you mean by *control*?" He didn't cut me off often, but when he did, he was generally onto something.

My elbows on my knees again, chin in my hand, looking at him. I sat back, shrugged, and put my arms behind my head to think.

"I don't know."

But I would find out.

Knowledge alone is insufficient for renewal.

Chapter 15

Talk Is Cheap

I HAD TOLD myself all the Truths I was supposed to believe in the hopes they'd save me. They didn't. And I had pretended to keep it all together, until I broke down in front of Raymond.

Why?

After a few months, Raymond and I meet less. No bad blood, just needing it less and less. But it's hard for old dogs to learn new tricks, and living with even some of my heart often left me confused. Shaky. Like learning to walk for the first time.

I was out for a walk in the university grounds, one of my favorite places to be in the city. The buildings were inspired by Oxford and Cambridge, and so through Queen's Park and along the sidewalks and cobblestone of the campus I'd wander, looking at the enormous arched windows, the stone pillars, and ornate spiers. As close to England as I had ever been. I had a few beers in my backpack—old habits die hard—and was planning on smoking a few cigarettes, my other misdemeanor, alongside them and trying to map out what came next in my life. It was a cool evening and I sat down on the grass in the courtyard of Knox College. There was a lot for me to reflect on. This wasn't the turning over of a new leaf; it was a full-scale life demolition and rebuilding. I didn't know how to take the first step.

Do I just start telling everyone what I feel all the time?

The sun slowly hides behind the skyline and sets the early evening sky ablaze. It's the dark reds and soft purples of dusk, and my bag is packed up with the empty bottles, and a lit cigarette is in my mouth as I begin walking home. And as fate or providence would have it, I bump into some friends I haven't seen in a few months. One last drag on the cigarette, a flick and a stomp, and then we're all walking together. The handshake-hugs, the exchange of pleasantries.

"How's therapy been?"

Word *does* travel fast.

The question hit me—hard. The bite of it in my chest, and the jitters through my hands. *Embarrassment.* That I couldn't control how I looked; that I was the kind of person who needed therapy.

"It's been good," I say. "Helpful." And then adding onto that, "There's tons of research into [insert whatever banality I said here]."

And there I had it.

Back to the same old ways of hiding behind my knowing.

What would Raymond say to all this?

He'd tell me I don't need to hide, that knowing didn't have to be a smoke screen for all my feelings. And I'd tell him he was right, but it's easier said than done, and being seen for the first time comes with all kinds of new insecurities. Ones I didn't necessarily want to face. And he'd say, "I know, but you must face them."

And so we're all walking and my friends are supportive of the facts I share and they tell me to give them a call if I ever need anything. I say thanks and smile, and then my station comes up, and we all head our separate ways.

The streetcar shows up and its doors open as it comes to a stop. Grabbing the handrail and stepping up inside, my mind is on my own disparity, the incongruity of my life. I'm standing, leaning against a window, watching the city pass me by in so many neon signs and flashing lights. I experience the world through my body, but for all kinds of reasons—fear and insecurity seeming to be at the top of that list, the wondering if I'm worthy of love—I've reduced that experience to *thinking about* the experience. But that's not sustainable. Breaking down, weeping through the city on the way to Raymond's, that was proof my body demanded to be heard and valued.

I didn't know what was going to happen next, and I didn't know what it meant to use my body, to learn from it, to listen to it. But it was clear, in some sense, that I was already teaching my body, learning from it, but it seemed to be in all the wrong ways.

I can see my face in the streetcar window, a reflection, and it's like looking at the old me, some sort of translucent ghost, one I can see through. But the me I am, the one that's doing the looking, the one that's leaning on the window, that one doesn't seem real yet either.

I'm stuck in between.

I take my pocket journal out, thumbing through it, looking for some guidance, for something that will make sense. One of the pages is dog-eared, and I read: "The Owl of Minerva spreads its wings only with the falling of the dusk."[1]

Hegel said that.

And then I'm thinking that the only way to make sense of my old way of life is to leave it behind and to enter a new one. I had been so stuck looking and assessing, trying to rationalize every next step, but what I need is to *actually* change. To take wing.

I wanted to be who I was made to be; I wanted every bit of mediocrity and chaos that lurked in me to be rehabilitated. Transformed. I wanted to become. I didn't want rebellion and selfishness to be solutions to the agony of living, and I wanted to stand in the Bright Light of every promise my faith was supposed to offer. I had lingered too long in the gloom, too long in a kind of masked fragility, too long with excuses and rationalizations to cover up all my faults and failings. I needed to *follow* the Hidden Music.

We all do.

I'd spent so long believing the person could be reduced to only soul, and then I'd doubled down on that, thinking that the soul could be reduced to mere thinking and rationality. And now, I needed more. I needed to become Fully Alive.

We all do.

I needed to cross the threshold.

Out of one way of living and moving and having my being, and into another. It was a bravery I didn't know if I had—not one I could conjure up or invoke, not one I could fake. It was forced upon me, demanding a choice:

Cowardice or valor.

I did not want to settle; I did not want *out*; I did not want to be remembered as cowering and fearful by my wife and everyone close to me. I would remain.

That 501 Queen streetcar is the longest route in the city. If I really needed some time to myself, I'd hop on and ride it back and forth. I always carry a journal, something to scribble thoughts into, write phrases, couplets, whatever was going on in my mind and life. Sometimes, like tonight, I'd write. A seat frees up near the back, facing out toward the scratched windows, and I'm taking my journal out. People rush and crowd in all around me, and it offers a kind of solitude. Order in the midst of chaos. I lean my journal on my knee, I click my pen, and then I let it all out. Some of it was questions, some of it was trying to figure out what came next—but as I settled, I wrote a poem. I still come back to this, every few months or so, not because it is some erudite work, but because it still wakes in me the feelings that marked the new days I was facing:

> When you walk off the compass
> and the rose has lost north,
> I could sing to you of marble trust
> and we can both march forth
>
> The night is dark, the road is long
> the wolves here offer no support

You can lean on me, my back is strong
and we can both march forth

This unknown land has a secret wood
the brave here made a fort
We call them slaves, those who stayed and stood,
but we can both march forth

Now we venture in uncharted lands
and by the sea there's a port
Looking back from these distant sands
we see that long lost north.
Oh, my chest has this journey's brand
since we both lost north—
across the sea now, just take my hand
and we will both march forth

I was not afraid.
I was hopeful.
I would walk on water, across the sea, into a new way of Life.

Sainthood is nourished by courage,
do not make decisions out of fear.

Chapter 16

Strong in Broken Places

IT'S EASY TO assume life is just one epiphany after another. Riding the highs every day, struck by the continual inspiration of the Muses. Unraveling all the secrets of the universe. But reality is a lot more severe than that. Epiphanies aren't like gumball machines—a quarter in, a twist, and watch them drop into your hands. Insights swell and subside like a tide; they come and go—based on so many cycles of living. Most of my days were the travail of tears.

The slog.

The reality about journeys like these ones, of leaving Rock Bottom, is that we still have to live our lives in the midst of it all. We still have to make money for rent and food, still have to sleep, still have to do all the *stuff* of life. There is no special reprieve for existential dilemmas. Life is often a catch-22, where it feels like no matter what we choose, we lose. Never enough time. Never fast enough.

I had the naive hope that those who peddled salvation as a product, the product that would change my life in an instant, were not lying. I wanted this whole journey to be done in a weekend. Take the first steps, hard as they were, and have everything else added unto me. *That'd make sense, right, God? Surely, in Your Grace, You'd honor the months of effort and reward me with a new spirit—a new lease on life.* A freshness and excitement. The gumball machine for my soul. And it was naive. Sincere, at least, when I look back. But it was wide-eyed and unaware. What I didn't know then, and what I know now, is that some things can only be learned on the itinerary of Time. We cannot grow a tree in a moment of passion, and the pathway through the Valley of the Shadow of Death has no signposts; there is no map. We must follow our Guide.

All of this to say, my day-to-day was still ordinary and grueling. The exhaustion that comes from hope deferred, the incongruity between expectations and the reality in front of me. Delivering food night after night. I was stuck in-between. No longer who I once was, but not who I wanted, who I anticipated I'd be. Things were not going according to schedule.

My wife, Aislinn, is the rarest kind of person alive—the kind of person who loves truly and deeply. They say love is wanting the Good of the other above the Good of self, and she wanted to see me through this. She wanted to see me whole and healed, to see me become who I desired to be; she wanted my Good even though it put us in all kinds of hard and harsh situations. It was real. And it was hidden, just for me, and just between us. It wasn't a love that demanded to be seen, but one that went through the Valley of Shadow with me. And that was Dostoevsky, shaping my understanding, opening my eyes to understand:

> Love in action is a harsh and dreadful thing compared with love in dreams. Love in dreams is greedy for immediate action, rapidly performed and in the sight of all. But active love is labor and fortitude.[1]

It was her active love, the commitment and the endurance, that got me through. Giving up is easy, making excuses is painless, but to endure? That's where the Life lies. And Aislinn taught me that.

We'd go for walks through the city every night, often stopping in at cafés or pubs or patios, to sit and chat. It was in the bleak December, the biting cold and the long nights. We'd crunch through icy snow on sidewalks, we'd window-shop, we'd hold mittened hands, we'd talk about everything I was going through. That was another bitter pill to swallow. I had wanted to believe that all of this, all of my choices, all of where those choices led me in life, only affected me. That only I had to bear the consequences. But on nights like those, nights where I could see her smiling face, see her bright eyes, I knew better. I knew that everything I did, both for Good and not, was not done in isolation, and that the myth of a solitary life was exactly that—wishful thinking. It was not Good for me to be alone, but it was also not Good to be with me in my current state. I had to be better.

We all do.

I have a picture from around this time, one I look at often, of Aislinn sitting in our favorite pub. We took our usual spot by the fireplace and ordered some ciders and cocktails and appetizers. One thing you need to know about my better half is that she is fiercely herself. "Most people are other people. Their thoughts are someone else's opinions, their life a mimicry, their passions a quotation."[2] Not so for her. People who love truly and deeply, and people who are themselves, with all wild passion, are about as rare as they come. And it is in these rare people we must place our trust—for often they are the only ones who see clearly, while the rest of us are content with various degrees of blindness, the kind of blindness that makes us feel good. They have heard the Hidden Music, while most of us remain deaf, the kind of deaf that absolves us of responsibility. Rare people are a gift, but one we often disparage. Their clear sight, their almost prophetic voice, unmasks even the most covert of us, leaving us bare and naked, facing the world as stark and vulnerable as the day we were born.

And our bodies teach this, that we cannot understand ourselves in isolation. We can't see the back of our own head, and so if we want to understand our whole person, we need *another*. We need the clear sight of community.

Our drinks came and we cheersed to Love and Life. Music played. And with a flick of her hand and a few magic words, we were talking about everything, all the unseen things, about not knowing who I was, about feeling worthless, about the regret, thinking I made a mistake in starting this whole thing, about how much it impacted her and my relationship with her.

"Those are always the questions," she said. "Who we are and where we fit and who we want to be."

Those are identity questions. The questions that put muscle and sinew and flesh on the bare bones of our existence. I had felt consumed, as by a fire, in starting this pilgrimage, reduced to only my skeleton—a weak and frail husk.

"That's the first step," she said.

She was right.

I couldn't expect a lifetime of mediocrity, of not feeling like I was enough, to wash away over a few months. There are no quick fixes for identity crises, and anyone who tells you different is selling you something. But this *was* something—I took a step, and whether by tripping or by intention, I managed to take others. I had torn down just about everything that didn't make sense in my life, everything that didn't line up with who I longed to be. Knocked down the whole house of cards. Woven cotton paper won't do for the storms of life; we need brick and mortar.

There's the trepidation of doing this, of taking the first few steps out of the pit and into the Wilderness, but you must do it. You cannot settle, and there's no such thing as standing still. And trust me, having the whole house of cards come tumbling down doesn't feel nice. But you know what's worse? Being washed away in the storm. Being shipwrecked, just waiting to drown. You will either take steps further up and further in, or you will descend, as I had, into the Graveyard, that place of the dead.

But those first few steps, they're a storm. The elements and weather feel coarse against the skin. We stand naked before the gale when all our walls are torn down. We are tempted to cower before the squalling rain, to turn and run. But we must not. We must stand and face the tempest. Alone. We must shake our hair and demand witness of the Lord of the Storm. We must roar out against all that seeks to capsize us.

We must endure.

We must rebuild.

We must always choose Life.

> The world breaks everyone and afterward many are strong at the broken places. But those that will not break it kills. It kills the very good and the very gentle and the very brave impartially. If you are none of these you can be sure it will kill you too, but there will be no special hurry.[3]

We must become strong in the broken places. It's not easy; our lives hang in the balance. But that was what I learned that night by the fire, sipping on old-fashioneds with my Rare person. I learned that all strength comes from healing the broken places. We often break, and some of us, beyond repair. But while there is breath in our lungs, we can stand before the storm. We can endure. We can overcome.

Grace is sufficient;
strength is made perfect in broken places.

Chapter 17

Divine Juxtapositions

THAT NIGHT, THE one with Aislinn and some drinks by the fire, was an oasis in a desert. I still had a lot to figure out, the same questions on repeat. One of the nagging doubts that lingered in my mind was who I wanted to be. Not something that can be answered easily. I knew that if I settled, if I answered the question too hastily, or if I didn't *really* believe it, it'd only be a matter of time before I found myself drowning in the bottom of a bottle, shored up in the pit. I needed something Big. Something Beautiful. Something that captured and captivated all of me. Something that made me more alive, ready to give up anything and everything to become who I was made to be: a Saint. I just needed to learn what that meant.

I know what it's like to read a book like this, to want to rush to answers, to want to quench the ache, to fill the void, to be able to say "and then," but this is different. This isn't the time to look for shortcuts, and the answers to all your deepest pains are not short sentences. That's the wrong way of understanding this *answer*. It is not a thought or platitude, a dogma or a phrase.

This answer is alive.

This answer is a Gate.

This answer is the Source of the Hidden Music.

A few months later Aislinn went to Arizona to visit some of her best friends, a yearly tradition. She'd be gone for just over a week; back to the bachelor life for me. Some of my friends at the church we were going to at the time, another new place, on the other side of the city, were having a whiskey night, and as a self-proclaimed connoisseur of the liquid sunshine, I agreed to go.

I caught the city bus down to my boxing gym, put in an agonizing ninety minutes, took another bus home, showered, grabbed a bottle of the good stuff off the shelf, bought myself a sandwich for dinner, and Ubered over to my friend's house.

"Don't get sloppy."

Aislinn's words to me before she left for Arizona. And I didn't intend to. I'd have two small tasters of the best whiskeys there and call it a night, sipping on soda water. Playing with fire and all that. Not wanting to get burned.

I went inside, dropped my bottle off beside the rest of them on the counter, and scoped out whatever I deemed to be top-shelf. I poured an ounce, not a heavy ounce, a legitimate one, and joined my friends. The air was thick, lots of bodies and laughter, and the wet humidity of radiator-heated Canadian homes cast fog on the windows. There were a few guys there I didn't know, so I introduced myself.

One of them was a filmmaker and photographer. We started talking about some of his projects, both past and ongoing, talked about all the stuff that makes cinematography work. I sipped away at my ounce, nursing it. The guy is telling me about composition and framing, and I'm swirling my drink, listening, and asking about how he found his eye for it all. A last sip, finishing my first ounce. *One more, and that's it.* I ask about lighting and storytelling, assure him I'm listening, and get up to pour another ounce.

I sit back down, and he's telling me about shadows and sources, about visual cues and emotion and sequence.

"That's how we get the story across," he says. "That's how people feel an image, or series of them."

I'm nodding, taking mental notes, sipping at my tumbler.

The next thing I hear is the thunderous steps of kids running through the house. I hear the giggling, and it's resounding in my ears. My eyes slowly peel open; I sit up, pained, vomit stains on my chest. The reverberation of my heartbeat in my head is an earthquake. I strain and stretch my neck. Nausea erupting in my gut. I see my friend, the guy who hosted, and he's frying up breakfast for his laughing, screaming kids.

"Good morning," he says.

I nod, eyes dull and heavy, and he walks over, asking if I'm okay.

"I don't know," I say. "What happened?"

"You blacked out."

He keeps explaining, but my hand goes up—equal parts not interested and queasiness. I do not care what happened. No need to add insult to injury. There's enough sickness and embarrassment swirling around in me, no need for the fine print.

I say thanks for taking care of me, and I put on my shoes and call an Uber. I throw my jacket on when the car pulls up. It's 7:00 a.m.

"There's a five-star review for you, and a tip, if you drive nice and slow and don't talk to me." The Uber driver nods in agreement.

We weave through the city, and it feels like my entire body is sloshing around in the back seat. The sun burns my eyes, the honking horns blare in my ears. Stereotypical hangover. Some fifteen minutes later and we're at the intersection of my apartment, so I tell him to stop.

"This is fine," I say.

The plan is a short stop at the corner store to buy something with electrolytes, and as I'm crossing the street in front of my Uber driver, waving, vomit erupts out of me. Some on his car. My hands palm together in front of me, the universal symbol for an apology, and I run into the store and grab a few bottles of coconut water. The first bottle is mostly done, fighting the protests of a swirling stomach, then it's a short walk up the street, unlocking the door beside the restaurant entrance, walk up the entryway stairs, open my apartment door, grab a trash can, and head to my room.

I sit on my bed, still a shaky mess, and cuss.

Not again.

Then it's time to sleep this off, as much of it as I can. I nap until just after one in the afternoon. I'm waking up to texts asking if I'm okay, asking what happened, all of which I ignore. Lying in bed, head still thundering from the dehydration, I order a bit of ramen, for the broth and the carbs. Another hangover secret. Soak up all the poison, get in more electrolytes. My head pounding. My stomach empty and rolling.

This is the worst hangover I've ever had, I'm thinking to myself. *Ironic that while I was drinking like tomorrow didn't matter, nothing like this happened, no blacking out. Try to quit though? Lights out.*

The rest of my afternoon was *Home Improvement* reruns on YouTube, spoonfuls of ramen, and the tiny sips of coconut water. Trying to stay still so all the chunks inside me stayed untossed. Someone had texted me a sermon. Even at the better times in my life, I wouldn't watch sermons in my spare time, and when I hit Rock Bottom, I watched them even less. There's this general disinterest in hearing any sermon save from my own local pastor. But for some reason, my finger tapped the link, and the voice is playing through my phone's speaker.

It was boring, nothing to really remember or write home about. But near the end, the sermonizer said something off the cuff, and not at all in line with his topic or train of thought.

"Lots of you have felt what it means to drift slowly." That was him, talking to me through my screen. "You've woken up one day and wondered how you got here; it wasn't where you wanted to go, but you barely noticed the aimlessness to your life. God wants you to know He sees you and welcomes you back."

It was short; it wasn't pithy or clever or eloquent. But it struck me. I had drifted. I had drifted down to Rock Bottom, and in this Wilderness I had wandered—ambled—aimlessly. And it led to black. Curtains. Roll tide. I order more ramen for dinner and then tune back into Tim Allen's masterpiece, but the thought of drifting never leaves my mind. Before bed, I called Ais and let her know what happened, how I only had two ounces and blacked out drunk. Neither of us has answers; neither of us understands.

Sunday morning comes and there is no real desire to go to church. Not for any bad reason, but because I didn't want my morning to be a dozen conversations about blacking out. Instead, I grab my journal and my backpack and head across the street to Starbucks. A black Americano and window seat and my journal, and I start writing. Trying to figure out the *drifting*. Needing to know everything I felt. Why I felt it. What even happened.

Was I ashamed?

I didn't want to get drunk; I didn't even want to feel a buzz, let alone black out.

I keep trying and I keep failing.

That's what my pen is scrawling out in my notebook. That's why I'm feeling embarrassed. I feel insane. Delirious. Like I'm doomed to walk this wilderness for forty years; like every choice made to be Good kept amounting to nothing. Like everyone was watching me flounder and ramble through all the darkest parts of my life.

Then it's the same feeling.

Not the nausea.

The heaviness and the swelling in my eyes and in my throat. The hot tears fill my eyes and roll down my cheeks. I'm crying. And I can't stop it. My body is demanding to be heard. I throw my journal and pen into my backpack and run across the street, run upstairs to my room, and weep. I'm leaning on my bed, sobbing.

The ugly kind. Alone in my room, bawling.

Pulling my hands from my face, they're filled with the wet of tears and sorrow, and then, I'm dreaming.

While awake.

A hallucination? A vision?

I see this precipice. I'm looking up at it from a purple, shadowed valley, its ridges illuminated by the soft glow of dawn. Squinting, trying to adjust my eyes. A Lion steps up, mane flowing in the morning breeze, silhouetted by the sun, and He looks at me. Golden eyes, a rich and shining amber. And He roars. It thunders. And in that moment, I feel the weight of everything. I feel the heaviness of all my *drifting*. But that's too small of a word. I feel the burden of all my rebellion—all my choices and decisions to be mediocre, to take my own path, to drink my problems away, to ignore them. Nothing was hidden; nothing could be hidden. No excuse could stand.

It's the weight of everything, and in this dream, I fall down to both hands and knees, head bowed. Being crushed to Death. A Death I'd flirted with just about every damn day of my life. My fingers strained, my forearms tensed, my shoulders taut and buckling. This was it. Exit stage right. But it didn't feel like I was to go peacefully into that long night; it didn't feel like rest was waiting for me. It felt like I would go the way I lived—descend farther and farther, beyond Rock Bottom, and into everything that comes when we try to unmake ourselves with rebellion.

I wanted one last look, to see those eyes, to see something Beautiful before it was all over, and at that moment, when I thought it was done, I was transported. Standing before the Lion, and weeping. I grab His mane, locks in each of my hands. I bury my face beside His and sob all the more. And I feel His paw reach around my shoulders and hug me closer, bring me nearer. And all the weight is gone, like Death wasn't lurking behind the corner, like the Grave couldn't swallow me up.

And I feel Love.

Then I'm in my room again, shaken out of the dream. Sitting beside my bed. Wondering. Wondering if it was real, if it actually happened, if this makes me a crazy person. And none of it really made sense to me. The same thoughts I assume you're having while reading this.

Was it real?

And I get that. It was my feeling too. At least rationally, in my mind. But my body?

It felt peace.

And it felt Love.

And it's hard for me to imagine anything more Real.

Ais came back the day after, and we go out to our favorite sushi place for dinner, just a few doors up from our apartment. We're seated by the window under some paper lanterns, and we order a platter for two. I tell her the whole story and we're crying together in the restaurant window, holding hands, knowing that God met me. It's the Divine Juxtaposition: Grace at the Bottom. The drawing near, the overlap of Heaven and Earth. The shape of Immanence. Hearing God and eating sushi.

Let me explain.

God is always speaking,
even at the Bottom; have ears to hear.

Chapter 18

Knowing God, Knowing Self

LET ME KNOW thee, O my Knower; let me know thee even as I am known."[1] That's what happened to me. We don't all need a vision to *wake up* (but apparently I did, me with my deaf ears and blind eyes); what we need is to have our eyes opened, we need to see. The Fathers and Sages and Wise men of all of Christendom have referred to this waking up as *knowing* God. But they don't refer to it as some mere intellectual enterprise. We don't know God by mere fact. We need to see Him, experience Him, enjoy Him. Not just in our heads but with our whole selves, body included. This is what I was learning, and it needed a bit of parsing out.

God is always speaking to us, and all gentle urgings, all of those Divine Interruptions, they matter. We tend to compare and contrast, make all kinds of value assessments based on scale and power; that a vision must be different than the impressions that happen from a daily reading. But all of God's leadings are of the same caliber. It is still the infinite, the Transcendent, stepping into the finite, drawing near, and revealing Himself.

It's not a stretch to say that often our desire to know Christ *only* by facts hampers our ability to see Him and experience Him, just like missing the kiss by all kinds of experimentation and hypothesis testing. What we all need are glimpses, peeks into more of His Fullness.

"For now we see through a glass, darkly; but then face to face: now I know in part; but then shall I know even as also I am known."[2]

There is so much that obscures our vision, so much that clouds our ability to see God clearly. It can be the fathers and mothers we were born with; it can be church hurt and abuse; it can be a culture so focused on self we do not remove our eyes from the reflective waters, like Narcissus of old. It can be fear, insecurity, addiction, or hypocrisy. But all of us have scales on our eyes, and all of us need a healing touch to have them drop.

Jesus, so we are told, did a lot of work during His time here, healing the blind so they would be able to see. And I used to wonder why He seemed to have switched gears so dramatically in our own time. Then He made me see. And it all began to make sense. We can be blind in more than one way, and we can see in more than one way. And usually, all the ways we want miracles are just that—what *we* want. I wanted to be out of the pit so I could keep going about life *my* way. I wanted Jesus' healing as a means to an end. But that won't do, and that's not what Jesus is about. Jesus is always, so He said, about His Father's work; and He is still healing the blind, the sick, the deaf, the mute, the broken, the crippled—healing them in the deepest ways.

This was the beginning of my grasp of my self—the whole person, heart, soul, mind, and strength. Both soul and body. God showed me Himself, as Loving and Protecting, and it revealed more about myself than I had ever yet imagined. Seeing Him, even through a glass darkly, shone all sorts of light on my path. I saw myself and the world as He sees us. Well, not fully but a bit more truly. And then it's a whisper of another voice from pages read some years before, another guide on this path I was on, helping me understand. It's Julian of Norwich:

> For some of us believe that God is Almighty and may do all, and that He is All-Wisdom and can do all; but that He is All-Love and will do all, there we stop short.[3]

It had been easy for me to know the might of God and the wisdom of God, but to know, in my soul and in my body, that God was Love—that seemed too much. I needed to be healed from a blindness, and to do so, I needed to behold. We all need to behold, to see more clearly, to interpret Life and living with respect to True Reality, which is the World as God made it and intends it, where His ethics reign and His Kingdom is the standard.

Seeing and *beholding*, especially in light of my vision, or dream, or whatever it was, can be terms that confuse. And I want to make it clear that there are ways to behold, to see, just as clearly in your every day, not just with so-called visions. To see God's provision in the breath in your lungs, to see His care in the blood in your veins, to know His pleasure in every laugh, to hear His voice in everything that is Beautiful.

That is the drive of all humanity: To see clearly. To see more and more. To behold and be transformed. That is the foundation of Sainthood. *Beholding.* Saint Gregory of Nyssa taught me that *beholding* is the desperate attempt to quench the longing for Beauty by beholding the Source of all Beauty. In seeing God, we *need* to see more; His Majesty creates in us a deeper and deeper longing—to be consumed and to be captivated. To have kindled within us a fire that cannot be extinguished:

> This truly is the vision of God: never to be satisfied in the desire to see God. But we must always, by looking at what we can see, rekindle our desire to see more. Thus, no limit would interrupt growth in the ascent to God, since no limit to the Good can be found, nor is the increasing of desire for the Good brought to an end because it is satisfied.[4]

I needed to be a person who saw God, continually, and then be transformed by that vision. To become like Him.

To become a Saint.

Only in beholding Jesus is all blindness healed.

Chapter 19

A Phenomenology of Sainthood

I KNOW HOW most minds work, not because I'm some soothsayer, but because we're all more alike than we are different. I know it doesn't quite feel *enough* to say that our identity is in the beholding. That feels too far off, intangible. We want the answer of our identity issues in our hands and in our mouths, to taste them and see them. To experience them the same way we experience everything else around us: in and through our bodies.

Most of my life had been spent with those esoteric and cerebral answers; I needed this answer in and through my body. I needed to know it in ways that a mere definition would not satisfy. If pictures are worth a thousand words, then a kiss can fill a library. And I wanted to understand what it meant to be a Saint the way I enjoyed a kiss, not by empiricism but by encounter. I wanted to know what it meant to be a Saint by consumption and union.

I wanted a phenomenology of Sainthood, a philosophy by experience. I didn't want to understand the Saint by science or scrutiny but by a kind of participation, a nearness. The thing is, from my understanding, Saints don't really announce themselves. No pomp, no circumstance. Unassuming, or better yet, meek, that's the name of their game. Finding a Saint wouldn't be easy. There were things, different things, to look out for. Before all this, I would have been looking for a certain set of criteria, the same kind of external manifestations that had marked my ever-so-mediocre life. But that wasn't going to work anymore. What I needed was a new way of seeing people and the world, and a new way of evaluating that which was Good.

There was this guy I had met at a Bible study a few years previous. He'd rolled in with the wind; he knew the pastor yet never attended the church. He was rough, had the edges most of us wished were sanded down; he was gritty. He'd come to the Bible studies we led maybe once a month. His white hair was long, parted, and his hands were always grease-stained; his face was etched with wrinkles, and it was sharp, and his eyes glowed a bright blue. He was thin, wore blue jeans, a black bomber jacket, probably late sixties, and always carried around a tattered leather Bible. The first week he walked in, he sat beside me, and before we started, he asked if I had ever been to Alcoholics Anonymous—almost like he knew what was coming. He told me he had been going for a long time, told me he had a sponsor and that he was a sponsor. He told me that the only way to love people was to know them, to share with them, to be open with them, and to have them be open with you.

"How else do you know what you're lovin'?" he asked.

Every time he'd show up at study, he'd share exactly where he was at—not in some morose or somber tone but with a bit of a smile, with a bit of hope. It wasn't bragging; it was like he had a joy in confessing, like he knew where confession led, and was happy enough to start the journey all over again. Like it didn't matter what we thought about him, like he only cared what God thought about him. After study we'd chat on the sidewalk, late, under streetlights. It was then he'd tell me of his love for fixing bicycles; about the shops in town he would volunteer at and teach people how to replace broken chains, fix brake lines, and insert inner tubes. He loved it.

"I've gotta get my bike fixed up," I told him. The months of delivery had taken a toll on my noble steed. And he invited me to the shop, and he prayed for me, and it was to the tune of the Hidden Music, and we went our separate ways. That's how things were with him, once a month or so.

Cycling home my mind is on my friend and all the *other* stuff he was into. Going to Alcoholics Anonymous, volunteering his time at the bike shop, and his genuine and joyful giving of his time and life to anyone who might need it. It wasn't just a kind of duty, a killing of sin. It was a Love and a pursuit of Life.

It was Divine Expansion.

Most of us, I've come to realize, live in the first half of the Christian mandate. We deny ourselves, we take up our cross, and . . . well, that's generally it. Life is no more than the denial of the bad, a rejection of all the rebellion within us. And that gets tedious and exhausting. It gets disheartening. I mean, it's the same bitter and arduous task day after day, because each of those days seem to push our buttons in just the right way to make us want to transgress. Surrendering the hopes, surrendering the dreams, putting everything about you to Death—that's what had caused so much fear in me. The idea that if I gave everything to Jesus, I would lose myself. I'd have to give everything up. And even though some of my impulses and passions were less than to be desired, they were still shadows of that which I longed for.

Would I lose all that too?

This perspective of self-denial is only half true. My view of self-loss was blurry at best. Somehow, on that bike ride home from Bible study, in the stories of my friend, I realized that self-loss was really about leaving a prison. The calls to deny self, to take up crosses, were in fact aimed at the *following*. "After all, almost the main work of life is to come out of ourselves, out of the little, dark prison we are all born in."[1] We come out and step *into*. That's the Divine Expansion. Not just some self-effacing flagellation but a harkening. A tuning of the ears to the trumpet call of adventure, the Hidden Music. "And the more I considered Christianity, the more I found that while it had established a rule and order, the chief aim of that order was to give room for good things to run wild."[2] That's what being a Saint was about: the *following*.

The surrender and the harvest. God was not a rival to my freedom. He wanted me to have it to the full.

What came for me, in the coming days and months and years, was a deepening and a broadening of all of this. A phenomenology of Sainthood is learned through a day-by-day participation. Of beholding, of following, of cooperation. Acquiring whatever definition I was looking for, longing for, required cultivation. I had to be planted and I needed to grow. In order to know myself I had to come to a growing knowledge of God—not simple facts or dogmas, but I had to know the joy of sharing in Him, even in His sufferings. What you may have already guessed is that for this, for a kind of living Love and Joy and Peace, there is no amount of language that can communicate understanding. Observing Saints, not just our heroes of old but also the Every Day ones, the ones that come to our Bible studies and volunteer their time to help the addicted, wakes something up within us. A further hunger. A hunger for more of the infinite Beauty of God—to follow Him further out of our little prisons and further into the Wild Expanse of His Kingdom.

That is the goal of all of life: becoming a Saint. That's what Albert Camus thought, at least—and even though he didn't believe in Jesus, I think he's right. He writes about this idea, the purpose of sanctity, in his book *The Plague*, a tale of a town ravaged by a cholera outbreak and a few who sacrifice just about everything to help the sick and dying. "I have no idea what's awaiting me, or what will happen when all this ends. For the moment I know this; there are sick people and they need curing."[3] That's the definition of a Saint, I think. And if you're paying attention, you'll see that there are no terms, nor are there any conditions. This isn't simply for the leaders of our churches, not simply for those who are farther along in years, in life, in anything. Not for those with some special pedigree or privilege. No, the definition, the invitation, is for all—at least everyone who is yet alive. It is for you, and it is for me. If you have eyes to see, then you, too, will see the sick people all around you—those who need curing. And who else will do it? That's the vision of the Saint: an Every Day person—normal and ordinary—doing all they can to *heal*.

"To become a saint, you need to live. So fight away!"[4] That's what hit me: an intentional living. A fight. It was deciding to embrace *every* moment as an opportunity to experience God by choosing to follow Him, up out of myself and further into His Goodness and Beauty. I had to be all in; and I decided then that I would not settle for anything less than *becoming* a Saint. That is who I was called to be, an image, or reflection, of Jesus, who was relentlessly about His Father's work. I needed to develop the same heart and soul and mind and strength.

In God's Reality there is True Freedom.

A LITURGY OF IMMANENCE

Faith demands renovation; Grace demolishes that which will not sustain.
Divine Love is not earned, it is a Gift freely given through prayer.
Knowledge alone is insufficient for renewal.
Sainthood is nourished by courage, do not make decisions out of fear.
Grace is sufficient; strength is made perfect in broken places.
God is always speaking, even at the Bottom; have ears to hear.
Only in beholding Jesus is all blindness healed.
In God's Reality there is True Freedom.

Act III.
The Architecture of Incarnation

Chapter 20

Following the Hidden Music

THERE REMAINED MUCH to figure out about what came next in the every day; a bike and a person needing takeout was only going to get me so far along in my five-year plan. And even though I was seeing more clearly, everything in my immediate life remained obscured. Where was the pillar of smoke to guide me by day? The column of fire to direct me at night? I didn't know what to do for myself or for my wife; I just knew we couldn't stay where we were forever. Everything has a shelf life, and hard seasons tend to spoil a lot faster than others. My life, my decisions, asked a lot of Aislinn; it's not only our bad decisions that demand much from those around us, so, too, does the pathway of renewal. Messes don't disappear in a moment, and often, the ones we love must shoulder just as much as we do. That was a truth that cut me; I wish I had figured more of this out *before* roping her into it all. She took it like a champ: the crammed quarters, scraping together just enough money to get by, the lack of direction and answers. It all began to add up. It's never the big things but the stacked-up little sacrifices that begin to erode who we are.

Throughout the spring we spent a lot of time planning. We had moved out of my old place and into her old place on the other side of town—a bit of a change, some more space and privacy, but still with roommates. We walked and talked every day, strolling through the neighborhoods of the city. Little Italy, the Distillery District, The Annex. We'd do the usual thing of grabbing something to drink and eat, and we'd share. We knew where we didn't want to be, but now the options before us seemed too broad. All these growing realizations gave the impression that *everything* now lay before us. The world was our oyster, all we had to do was jump in and take the pearl out. We threw out idea after idea hoping that something would stick, that something would make sense. There was no obligation to go back to a job I hated just because it provided. I used to call that wisdom. I saw now how much it destroyed me. So what came next?

It didn't take much thought to realize I needed help. I needed a bit of mentoring, to get under a wing, to find guidance. Real and embodied. There are these new steps we take, and we take them like infants, shaky and unbalanced. And as you think through your own new steps, into these embodied ways of living, of beholding, I'm urging you to find someone who can offer you help—not just by their support but by their example. Someone you can learn to live anew with.

Aislinn and I were continuing our rhythms of walking, talking, and figuring—night after night. Tonight, we're heading to a pub to have dinner with some leaders of the current church we are attending. These leaders had come to visit our church plant from England—that was ground zero for the movement our church was a part of. We had hit it off with them and had started going out together once a week to talk about life and the church and next steps.

We're in the pub, seated, waiting for food and drink to come, and I'm telling them a bit about my hope for mentorship.

"I think I need some guidance," I'm saying, "from the ground up. Intro-level stuff, patient and slow, to let me figure out how everything I'm learning makes sense in real life."

The beers come, none for me this time, and we all clink glasses and sip away, me at my water.

"Come to England," he says, sipping at his beer. "The church we go to has a great mentorship program."

Which seems out of left field, and it was, but it was something we were able to seriously consider.

"I'm not interested in a program," I say. "I don't want to come and *have* to be someone; I just want to find someone who I can figure out my life with. To just do life, in the most normal way possible, and to reimagine it—rebuild it—on the right foundation."

And they say, the leaders, the husband and wife, almost in unison, "We know a few couples who would love you guys."

It had been about a year since I'd quit my job at the bank, about a year of cycling through the city delivering food, about a year of tightening the proverbial belt, about a year of just scraping by. And, as crazy as it sounds, when we got home after that invitation to England, and when we crunched the numbers, it was cheaper to leave our city and live abroad. Ais decided to pick up work teaching English as a second language online, and I started doing design and art commissions. And that was all the extra push we needed, on top of the prayers and our trusting those leaders had our best in mind.

We packed up our entire life, selling as much as we could, putting the rest into storage, each with only a suitcase and backpack for the journey; we bought one-way tickets and flew off to jolly ole England.

I want to make sure you don't hear what I'm not saying. This isn't a how-to manual—I'm not suggesting jobs get quit, you drink yourself comatose, and pick up and leave the country. I'm asking you to listen to the Hidden Music and to have courage enough to follow it wherever it may lead. This is what it took for me, but not all of us have the same journey. That's part of what it means for Good things to run wild—that's part of God's Divine Expansion. Each of us has the same goal in mind—Sainthood—but the paths are not the same. My friend, the man with the bright blue eyes from Bible study, his path was Alcoholics Anonymous and fixing bikes; Aislinn's path, at least in this season, was supporting me through the pain, hearing the Hidden Music as it sang to her of unconditional love. All my heroes—Lewis, Chesterton, Dostoevsky—they all had their paths too. And so do you. But you must listen and pay attention to all the ways in which God is speaking to you, beckoning you further up and further in. And you must have courage to take every step necessary.

Surrender, by listening, to the Way of God.

Chapter 21

The Long Obedience in the Same Direction

OUR FIRST DAY in the UK was stereotypically rainy and the rows of houses were brick and as we walked, looking for a place to rent, we stopped into cafés and pubs—places to dry off and warm up. For the time being, we were staying with the aunt and uncle of one of our friends from Toronto; which, looking back, was probably part of their path into Sainthood. They offered us a place to stay as long as we needed; the open doors, the open hearts, and genuine hospitality—all Hidden Music.

Some of the cafés were older than my country, and as we sat at a table, coffees in hand, I took in my surroundings. The hardwood floors were knicked and edged, none of the tables matched, the stone walls were crumbling, and there was patterned crown molding on the roof. I checked underneath our table, and there was a stamp: "Made in England," from some hundred and fifty years previous. And you could almost feel it, how *used* that table was—how many elbows had rested on it, how many plates or saucers or pint glasses had sat on top of it. How much laughter or how many tears or conversations were shared. It was marked by life and by time.

So it is with us. We are marked by life and time, and I was slowly learning the amount of time and effort a Good and godly life takes.

Information is not formation, and in our time of instant gratification, we tend to settle for whatever is easiest. We love the infomercials that sell us the body of our dreams by drinking some magic potion. We love the get-rich-quick schemes. We do the same thing for our walk with God—we take the easy way out. We feel this moment of passion, we feel this flurry of excitement, this deep conviction, and we set into fixing it all. We buy the latest and greatest thing for our hearts, devour it over a weekend. Push-ups for the soul. Crunches for our study. Sprints for our ethics. An ardent spurt of work, and we are disheartened when we flex in the mirror and still see tiny biceps. Our entire spiritual walk is still weak. But if I wanted to bear the marks of Sainthood, like that table, it would take time. And God makes everything beautiful in its time.

Formation isn't instant.

There are no shortcuts or easy ways out. I wanted to be a Saint, and so I needed to embrace the path. The "long obedience in the same direction,"[1] the slow transformation from seed to sapling to, hopefully one day, mighty oak. The hardest part of this for me was a change of mindset. Growth was previously measured in tangible, incremental ways—ranging from information acquired to following lists of dos and don'ts. It could be explained on a chart, checked-off boxes, and by comparing to others. That wouldn't be the right way going forward—I wasn't after external markers. I wanted an internal revolution. I needed to see my life as an opportunity and an offering. It would need to be the nitty-gritty stuff, the behind-the-scenes stuff, the stuff we cannot fake, and then just let the chips fall where they may.

What does that mean?

What am I going to do?

Jesus said that "unless a grain of wheat falls into the ground and dies, it remains alone; but if it dies, it produces much grain. He who loves his life will lose it, and he who hates his life in this world will keep it for eternal life. If anyone serves Me, let him follow Me; and where I am, there My servant will be also."² The Death part, the dying to self, as it were, was easy. But the harvest? The loving? The following? That didn't make any sense to me at all.

If becoming a Saint was the goal, then the plan was planting a Good Life. It would take time, that I knew; I just didn't know the way. There were my old ways of serving and following, but simply doing the same things scared me. I didn't know if they would land me in the same mediocrity I was in before, if the path ended at Rock Bottom.

I wasn't looking for a map, though—because none of us take *quite* the same journey. What was needed was a direction and some guidance, a *how*. Someone to give me a shake and reorient me if things got out of hand, if I strayed too far. This wasn't about being a maverick, about pulling myself up by my own bootstraps, or the arrogance of thinking I knew best. I needed to learn to own this new way of Life, to take responsibility for it. I alone would give an answer for how I lived, and no one else would be my excuse. It was a step of courage. One where I helmed the direction of my living, maybe for the first time. I alone would bear the weight of my decisions, not pass them off onto whoever told me to live a certain way. I just needed direction, to see the *inside* of someone's life.

Think about it for a moment. Jesus modeled His way of Life for three years to His disciples; He let them see the inside of His life. And when we read the Gospels, we are along for the ride; we see all the ways His life didn't make sense with theirs, we see the clash of *how* reality was interpreted. How confused and blind the disciples were to Jesus' way of being. And continually, Jesus met them where they were at, shaping and breaking off, rebuilding and reorienting. His goal was to give them new eyes, a new heart, to lead those who follow Him into the Fullness of His Life.

We went to a prayer meeting at the church suggested to us by our friends—the ones who had invited us to England in the first place. It was our second night, a Friday, and a few people were told that some Canadians would be darkening the doorstep, and they were probably encouraged to give us a warm welcome. We went in, shook some hands, said some hellos, made a few jokes about going to the "Motherland," and sat down for the service. Which was beautiful. Singing, prayer, sharing with one another—it felt like a family. Two hours later, when the service wrapped up, everyone was invited to the local pub for a drink. We gladly took up the offer and walked over to The Stag's Head with a few of the people we had just met. We get there, and a leader in the church was buying the first round for *everyone* who had joined. We were a bit late, so he pulled me aside and asked what kinds of beer I liked.

"IPAs," I tell him.

And he said I might as well have one from the country they were invented in.

A pint of his favorite.

Some of me accepted the pint to be polite, some of me accepted it because I wanted it, and then most of me wondered if, somehow, I could enjoy a draught without abusing it, if I was in a place where I didn't "need" it to survive.

For the next few hours we're all laughing and telling stories, enjoying the Fullness, arms around each other, smiles and hugs and genuine affection, and then we all make our way home. And something about that night, the two hours of prayer previous and the few hours of merrymaking after, opened something up inside me. It was different from what I had experienced before, different from my previous shame-filled mindset. This was a two-handed grasp on "spirituality," one that understood both body and soul, one that could kill sin and then experience the Divine Expansion.

I knew part of it, the killing the sin, the list of to-dos, but the Divine Expansion was harder. Why? I had been looking at my life with one eye closed—my perspective was skewed and distorted. If I was going to see clearly, I'd need both eyes open; partial blindness will not do.

That night I was shown what I was missing. I had read and been shaped by John Owen's *The Mortification of Sin*—a four-hundred-page treatise on how the *entirety* of the Christian walk is no more than a war against the self. We have these ongoing tendencies, John would say, these inclinations, this depravity, and just about every moment of every day was going deeper and deeper into the war. Even our good deeds, a cup of cold water to those who thirst, are probably riddled with selfishness and desire for glory. Sin was in us, on us, all throughout us; our every desire, so I read, and so I was taught, was the same kind of narcissistic rebellion of the first humans in Eden.

There were, to be sure, a few amendments made to Owen's tome, people adding in some thoughts and clarifications—one of which is this concept of *vivification*. If *mortification* is the putting to death, then *vivification* is the bringing to life. One a subtraction, and so we would assume the other was an addition. My experience was a bit different, however. Vivification was defined, in the books and sermons I had read, as a kind of living unto God. Sounds good, but when push came to shove and we tried to figure out exactly what that meant, it ended up being no more than *put sin to Death*. Sure, it would get dressed up in other phrases, other language—walk in newness of life, be holy, live righteously. But how did you walk in newness of life? Put sin to Death. How did you be holy? Put sin to Death. How did you live righteously? Put sin to Death. Two sides of the same coin, but each side had the same face on it.

Somehow, watching that leader buy everyone a pint shook me up just enough to open my other eye, to have my perspective aligned. It's not like I had never seen kindness before, not like I hadn't seen generosity, or a kind of largesse that lays a foundation for all kinds of laughter. It was the contrast and context that knocked the scales from my eyes. It was the nearness and farness of it all. The fact that many pints and many prayers could be enjoyed so near to each other seemed to cure a blindness in me. This was body and soul; this wasn't generalities of Goodness. This was overflow into celebration.

There's these short phrases Jesus uttered, about when an unclean spirit leaves a person, it goes out to the wild and desolate places, trying to find some rest. Finding none, the unclean spirit decides to go back "home"—and when it returns, it find the house empty and swept up, all in order. This clever devil then goes out, getting a gang of seven other devils more wicked than himself, and together they enter the person. Jesus said that this person, who emptied and swept up, is now worse off than before.[3]

I had felt that, felt the emptiness and the temptation to more evil. The cutting off, letting go, the attempt to sweep up, saying no to coping mechanisms—but in their place came other temptations, other ways to numb the pain or find solace. For me, as I'm sure you've picked up, there was the anger and the apathy, there was the bitterness and the temptation to blame. Those don't seem as sinister as being drunk before work, but bitterness is just as effective as drunkenness when it comes to unmaking, to self-destruction. When it comes to blindness and deafness to the Hidden Music. I had cleaned out some of the mess, and since nature abhors a vacuum, all kinds of fury and ire came rushing in. I had put to Death, but I hadn't brought in new Life.

My living was one-eyed, all soul and no body, and I staggered on the path because of it, blindsided by so much. But then there was that prayer meeting and that pub, and somehow my other eye opened. It was what I was looking for: something beautiful and embodied. It wasn't enough to keep emptying the house, to keep putting my mess in order; I needed to furnish my life. I needed a hearth, I needed tables and chairs, I needed rugs and art. I needed to build a life, a full Life. By *full* I mean embodied and real, I mean touchable and tangible, I mean it in the sense of incarnation. A spirituality in the flesh. I didn't just want to know about love, I wanted to experience it and share it, not simply with thoughts and words but with generosity and laughter and touch. I didn't just want to know about peace, I wanted peace in me and to burst forth from me when all the storms of life came. *Full* means body and soul, head and heart, all of you, to the extreme.

The full person, body and soul, is an offering; obedience is momentum.

Chapter 22

The Blueprint of a Saint

THE PATH OF the Saint leads into Fullness. Not Fullness in some undefinable cloud; Fullness as in the place where all longings lead; to hear the longings, both body and soul, and to run toward the Source. Becoming a Saint was to join that path—it was to follow them, those who had gone on before me. "Follow the saints, because those who follow them will become saints."[1] Thanks for the tip, Clement of Rome. If I wanted to become a Saint, I would need to walk in their way. But not because *they* were the goal. They were on their way *toward*, and I wanted that too. Up out of and farther *into*. And it was easy to follow them, for they left footprints, left holy little *messes* everywhere they went. Disturbances. Flipped tables. Melodies of the Hidden Music.

I spent as much time as I could reading about the Saints and the Fathers and Mothers of the church. My goal wasn't memorization, it was familiarity. It was hoping to pick up the threads that marked all their differing journeys—that which united them across all their diverging experiences.

Virtue.

That was their living, in essence. And all those virtues could be summed up even further: Love. Love was the mark of their lives. It couldn't be reduced to mere duty; though, so much of what they wrote and lived was an intense discipline and a relentless obedience. It seemed to me that in their view, obligation was a derivative of Love, not the other way around. Love will embrace a duty, it will shoulder the burden, and it will give everything. But Love is more than duty; Love will drive us to sing and dance and walk on water in the midst of the storms. Love frees us to live in ways that strict obedience does not oblige. Obedience goes no further than requirements; it stops at our bitterness or cynicism, crumbles at our angers and addictions. Love is at the center of all virtue, of all ethics. Paul said so. Read this with new eyes:

> And yet I show you a more excellent way. . . .
>
> Though I speak with the tongues of men and of angels, but have not love, I have become sounding brass or a clanging cymbal. And though I have *the gift* of prophecy, and understand all mysteries and all knowledge, and though I have all faith, so that I could remove mountains, but have not love, I am nothing. And though I bestow all my goods to feed *the poor,* and though I give my body to be burned, but have not love, it profits me nothing. . . .
>
> Love never fails. But whether *there are* prophecies, they will fail; whether *there are* tongues, they will cease; whether *there is* knowledge, it will vanish away. For we know in part and we prophesy in part. But when that which is perfect has come, then that which is in part will be done away.
>
> When I was a child, I spoke as a child, I understood as a child, I thought as a child; but when I became a man, I put away childish things. For now we see in a mirror, dimly, but then face to face. Now I know in part, but then I shall know just as I also am known.
>
> And now abide faith, hope, love, these three; but the greatest of these *is* love.[2]

Without Love, our virtue is merely a decision of the head, bound by that which must be done. Compulsory, rather than a Loving Pursuit.

This is *why* I struggled so much with all my aforementioned coping mechanisms—they were cravings I was unable to overcome because I had shut down the apparatus I needed to overcome them: my heart. Our time is one awash in promiscuity and all kinds of debauchery; bodies are used as means to our own ends. The battle for any kind of chastity (a virtue, mind you) is often lost because we forget that sex, and everything around it, is an act of love. It is a passion, in the philosophical sense, an instinct and a drive. If our virtue isn't marked by and rooted in Love, we will never subdue all those rebellious appetites. We fight fire with fire, except the fire of Love is eternal and burns hotter than the sun. The fire of Love consumes the fire of rebellion.

We become what we love.

The Saints loved Love. They loved the Source of all Love, loved it more than their whole lives. And they were transformed. Nothing would threaten them from their course—they were after Fullness, and so they *became* loving. Not like turning a new leaf. They began to *be*, as a state, a disposition. Each moment was an opportunity and invitation to *be*, to *become*. Obstacles are redeemed and become invitations—opportunities to display Love in the very moment we are most tempted to abandon it.

These invitations are both *out of* and *into*; they both *mortify* and *vivify*. They kill the selfish rebellions in us and they set Love to Life. That Love looks like virtue, the Good Life. When we say that we want to kill pride, we must learn to put humility to Life. The same goes for greed; we wage war against it with generosity. We battle lust with chastity. We contend against anger with patience. We strive against gluttony with temperance. We wrestle envy with charity. We combat laziness with diligence. It is a putting off *by* putting on.

But how do we *learn* virtue?

We need to get it *in* us, as a new sort of impulse:

> Learning virtue—becoming virtuous—is more like practicing scales on the piano than learning music theory: the goal is, in a sense, for

your fingers to learn the scales so they can then play "naturally," as it were. Learning here isn't just the information acquisition; it's more like inscribing something into the very fiber of your being.³

We want the impulse of our hearts to be one of Love, and in that sense discipline is freedom.

Virtue is about teaching our bodies to Love.

Take Confession, in its most broad and general sense. A person will go to see their priest, confess their rebellions and faults, and the priest will recommend they say however many prayers, or paternosters, and the priest will absolve them of their sin. And I used to think that was a missed mark; there aren't any amounts of prayer that can absolve the deeds done. But that's not the goal, or at least the only goal. Confession is also a new and embodied liturgy. It is to have the prayers so deep in the heart and soul and mind that when faced with any trial or temptation, the impulse slowly moves from *my will be done* to *Thy will be done*. It is a discipline of the body so as to teach the soul.

That is what it means to put on virtue, to bring it to Life. It's about embodied repetition, about decisions, and about destination.

Embodied Love is the path into all Virtue.

Chapter 23

"Now That You Don't Have to Be Perfect, You Can Be Good"

LIFE IS A lot slower than I had realized. Over the span of a few weeks we had packed up all we had and hopped continents; but days still roll by twenty-four hours at a time. It didn't take long for England to become routine, for us to find our groove and settle into it. We had made a few friends, and those friendships, by a Grace, went very deep in a short order.

One of my new friends, Ben, would invite me out for drinks at The York. I'd walk over from the flat we were renting and into the brick pub on the corner. The floors were herringbone wood, the walls were a paneled oak, and we'd order our pints at the bar, then head to our corner spot—leather benches and oak chairs. It was always the right amount of dark in there, the kind where no matter how many people were seated around you, it felt like home. It was late October and Ben and I had already hit it off, had our fair share of pints and conversations, and he had treated me to my first-ever British fish-and-chips. We had the kind of friendship that runs deep before it's ever superficial; less concerned with weather and daily comings and goings, and more concerned with all the stuff of Life. It was raining outside, and the droplets were catching the white headlights and red brake lights of so many passing cars. A thousand weaving prisms.

"You have to be who you were made to be."

Ben said that to me, and I said it right back to him, not as a "no, you" sort of thing, more like a "we're in this together" sort of way.

"It's hard because we see all the ways we're *not* who we should be—we see everything that disqualifies and invalidates. And still, the only way forward is becoming." He says that.

There was a rare pause in the conversation. I leaned onto the table, held my pint glass in both hands, and pondered. Ben was right. I wanted to be a Saint; he knew it, I knew it, and he wanted the same thing. But we also knew all the ways we weren't Saintly. I knew I was angry and apathetic and had a weakness for the drink; Ben knew his own Achilles' heels—but he saw more clearly than I did. He knew those weaknesses were the path forward, while I thought they disqualified me. He knew that despite everything that would make a person deride and jeer a gifting, a calling, a longing, the way remained the same: onward.

Whether he knew it or not, he put a lot of emphasis on the *-ing* when he said *becoming*; maybe it's just the accent of those in "the North," but it was a providential dialectical slip of the tongue. The present participle, the -ing words, express the action of a verb. The verb of my life was *to become*, and the *what* was a Saint. But it's the -ing that matters, the actions expressed. And therein lies all the beauty—the Beauty of Becoming. That's what I needed to capture and cultivate in my life: a vision for the beauty of the process. An idea that every day was part of the refining, that the slow days, the hard days, the ordinary days are just as magical and mystical as the momentous days. "Isn't it funny how day by day nothing changes, but when we look back everything is different."[1]

"You're right," I said to Ben. "And we're always moving forward, just not always in the right direction."

The Beauty of Becoming, for me, found its first steps of expression in Britain—Saintward bound, and learning to enjoy every moment as an opportunity up. We do always move, are always caught in the -ing of life—always expressing. "If you want to build a ship, don't drum up the men to gather wood, divide the work, and give orders. Instead, teach them to yearn for the vast and endless sea."[2] Most of what it meant to *become* was to learn a new way to Love, a way in which that Love swallowed up everything in my life; where I would do, could do anything to enjoy and experience that Love. Love, as a Source, becomes that which consumed my whole life; it became my destination, it fueled my virtues, and it is what drove me to find the charm in my every day.

The call goes out to all of us—to experience a Love that consumes us, that drives us to *become* who we were made to be. It's a call that demands the whole person, body and soul, and it's a call that we must listen to, seek to hear, and one we must follow. It is in the following that we are transformed; it is by taking the path of virtue that we *become*. You may take it, or you may not, that choice is yours—but I am telling you, your Life depends upon it.

Recapture the Beauty of Becoming.

Chapter 24

The Myth of Extraordinary

OUR FIRST WEEK in England we signed up for memberships at a local bouldering gym—rock climbing, if you don't know the lingo—about a thirty-minute walk from the flat we were renting. The seasons were changing, and our walks over in the morning were quintessentially British. Leaves had burned their reds, some had fallen and scattered the laneways. Stone walls lined the sidewalk, and iron gates fenced off entryways, and the smell of fireplaces rose and fell as we turned corners. The air was damp, the gray clouds sat low, and we held hands as we talked. Our routine both so similar and so different. When we'd get to the gym we'd order some coffees, lace up our shoes, and climb the mornings away. I didn't know it then, but that gym was a veritable *mecca* for climbers—just about as good as it got. There was this two-fold beauty in our naivety: We didn't know anyone and they didn't know us.

Everyone was ordinary.

It didn't take long for us to make friends; head nods turned into hellos, and those turned into working on a climb together, and that slowly grew into texting to make sure we'd see each other at the gym. Some of our friends who climbed there were paramedics, others were videographers, some were professionals, and others did it as a hobby. In the gym, we all worked our hardest—some on harder problems, but each of us, respectively, at the brink of our strength and skill and courage.

There was this one climb Aislinn and I were working on; we couldn't figure out foot placement and kept falling off the wall going for the crux, the hardest section of the climb. Two women were on the bench watching us, getting their shoes on, and one of them suggested we pivot, moving our weight from one side of our body to the other, switching feet, and then going for the next hold. And it worked like a charm.

We chatted with them for a bit while they warmed up and we finished our coffees. They knew from our accents that we weren't from England, so we shared some of what brought us there, and after about half an hour of conversation, we met up with some of our other friends.

"You know who that is, right?" they asked.

"No clue," we answered.

Turns out, the two girls were professional climbers; one competed all the time, and the other was her coach. A few years later, I'd watch her compete for England in the Olympics. But what amazed me then, and still does to this day, was how *ordinary* she was. We shared stories of our pets, and every time we saw her in the gym, she'd wave hello. She didn't know our stories, and how England was a searching for us, a trying to figure out our lives, and we didn't know her story; we just shared a gym and some coffees and conversations every few weeks.

It's hard for me to imagine that happening now, not because she changed but because culture has changed. People don't seem, or act, so ordinary these days. Everyone has this idea that they're on the cusp of celebrity, of being discovered, of basking in more than fifteen minutes of fame. Our time suffers from Main Character Syndrome: that the world is all ours and everyone else is just spinning in it. The notion of success, whether as a climber, or as an artist, or a ministry leader—or anything else—has boiled down to *celebrity*. The time of the ordinary person has disappeared, evaporated; all our heroes now need the bright lights and the red carpets.

It seems to have overtaken us quickly, this idea of being the main character, of being priority numero uno in our own lives; everyone else is "the help"—a like, a follow, or a supporting role in the production *Me*. Maybe it's because of phones, maybe it's because of so-called self-esteem culture, and maybe it's because we're all a bit selfish—whatever it is, it's completely transformed how we *do* our living. We live *for* now: for the eyes, for the attention, for the hopes of one day arriving. This is a liturgy that shapes our every moment, a public ritual that patterns how we go about everything we do. Being ordinary is a myth; everyone is *extra*ordinary now, sold on the lie that each of us will be a kind of celebrity, that we all deserve some kind of clout, that even our most mundane and prosaic tasks should be up on the stage for all to see.

Later that week I was standing at the back of the church auditorium, sipping on coffee in a paper cup, poured out from a steel carafe. This man comes up beside me and makes a joke about how the Brits do tea better than coffee. He has a traditional eagle tattoo on his forearm, white stubbled beard, and bright blue eyes. I tell him I hope so because the coffee isn't much to write home about. People are shuffling to their seats, music begins to play, and he tells us to sit with him and his wife. After the service he jokes that the people who suggested we move to England were paying them a pretty penny to befriend us; their camaraderie didn't come cheap.

Whatever the price was, we're glad it was paid. We were over to theirs for dinner often; have something homemade, or some kebabs, or anything, and we'd wash it down with coffees and teas and gin and tonic and hours and hours of conversation. Their fireplace was on, and after dinner we all moved to the living room, cozied up on couches. Jon, that was his name, was telling me about some ministry work he did, some of the training he had, and some of what he was currently working on. Aislinn and Kerry, that was her name, were talking about art and creating, seated closer to the fire. At that time, Jon wasn't a leader in the church we were attending, but he'd been involved in the church world for a very long time. The two of them, Jon and Kerry, were close friends with a *very* famous church person, who can remain nameless because that's the point of all this.

"We'd head back to the hotel we were staying at," Jon was telling me, "after a full day of teaching and mentoring and sharing, and we'd get coffees and have a heart-to-heart on the couches of one of our rooms. When we'd wind down for the night, he'd get up to leave, and it almost seemed like he could fit under the door, could leave without opening it, that's how little he thought about himself." And in these conversations, same with my friend Ben, I found a kind of *ordinary* mentorship. A learning by living and peeking into a life.

It was a humility that marked Jon's friend, never taking himself too seriously, never thinking of himself more highly than he should. It was anti-hype. A reverse celebrification of the person. An idea that even if a person was, in fact, extraordinary, they were still ordinary. The "mirror, mirror on the wall" didn't lie; it just showed a man of flesh and blood, like all the rest of us. And in a world of people desperate to be the fairest of them all, because beauty is a kind of power to be wielded, the ordinary person is the one who left the biggest impact on my friend Jon. And now has impacted me.

There's this idea lots of us buy into that in order to become *something* we need to first be *someone*. How can you become a Saint without a social media following? A pastor without going viral? A worship leader without an audience? Unheard of. So many of our best people—our artists and speakers, our singers and writers, our mothers and fathers, our husbands and wives, our friends, brothers, everyone—have this temptation to squander all that *ordinary* strength to the narcissistic ideal of being *extraordinary*. My generation was raised on the idea that nothing but success could come our way—be a doctor, play in the NHL, the sky was the limit. You can be a movie god, a rock star, the main character, but then life hits. And the whole parade comes to a crashing halt, and we realize that being extraordinary is mostly a dream, a myth; and the celebrification of our lives has done nothing more than separate us from what it actually means to be alive.

Living through the Mirror, Mirror disconnects us, separates us from Reality. There was a time when what we did, who we were, everything, was corporeal—embodied. There was no other way to interact with the world, we just had our bodies. Our lovers, our families, our friends—they were all the same: incarnate. Our hobbies, even, were physical, or at least substantial. When we wanted love, it was from another person sitting in front of us; we could reach out and touch them. But those times have passed, and even though we, the people, are real, we don't interact in a real way. We've been disconnected.

Instead of *being* our bodies—interacting and experiencing with them, finding identity through them—we do so, often, with our phones. Screens. Everything mediated to our minds via glowing pixels. The Mirror, Mirror that promises us everything. We have disembodied ourselves. Our needs, however, have remained the same: to love and be loved, to see and be seen, to know and be known. It's just that, now, instead of doing it *with* Real people through our bodies, we do it *for* virtual people—an infinite mass of potential likes and follows and adulation. It doesn't satisfy. It can't. It does the opposite. It starves us. Living as disconnected, as virtual, is a continual diminishing; a need to be loved, for real, and never experiencing it.

The myth of being extraordinary is slowly killing us. The lingering creep of Death, eroding what it means for us to be *truly* human. We keep asking who's the fairest of them all, hoping it's us, that in some way, we will be *enough* to be larger than life. But there's always someone, something else, some situation that turns all our moments into nothing more than normal. But that's the boon, the miracle, of being human, I think. Being able to walk under the door.

Ordinary.

And that, the every day, is a True Gift to humanity.

The Ordinary is Holy.

Chapter 25

You Will Be Forgotten

I GREW UP on a steady diet of celebrity. Even in the church. Tons of *what* I was supposed to be was wrapped up in the same sort of worldly view of distinction. We gather around the famous and notable, we laud prestige and prominence, and we have this view that following Jesus inevitably leads to *being* extraordinary. It wasn't explicit; it was hidden behind tons of ideas and catchphrases—a kind of hierarchy of success.

Years ago I was at a conference, one of those weekend getaways that promise to be solutions to the many ailments of a broken soul. In between the sermons and speeches, we'd spend time meeting and connecting with others, the Christian version of networking. I was invited by a professor of mine at the time to a special event, a catered dinner and a panel discussion on marriage and love and the gospel. It was a dress-up affair, but I had only packed jeans and hoodies and button-ups, and when I skateboarded over to the event, held in a kind of museum, I felt the weight of being severely peasant. I left my skateboard in the front lobby and headed in to do some mixing and mingling—meeting some pastors and leaders from churches all over North America and discussing all kinds of things about life and ministry. A few of us had grabbed our plates and were seated around a coffee table.

"It's all about legacy," one of them said in a thick southern accent. I'm eating some hors d'oeuvres, pâtés, and olives and crackers and cheese, listening to the back-and-forth. In agreement, someone else says, "That's why I'm building a ministry that's going to outlast me." And he starts talking about the impact of having too narrow a view, thinking that life is small and provincial, about how everything is *more* than it seems.

"How do you measure it?" I ask. "Legacy?"

There was a moment of silent thought, and then handfuls of answers came in from each of them, building and snowballing on top of each other.

"Numbers."

"Longevity."

"Cultural impact."

"Buy-in."

There was classical music playing through the speakers and there was the hum of just as many voices locked together in idea-sharing over plates of appetizers. Ours stayed the course, deepening the ideas of impact into strategies for expansion, best practices for future-proofing, staffing, and everything else. Making waves; being remembered. The event started, the emcee called us to the rowed seats near the front, and we heard a few people talk about how the gospel influences and impacts their marriages.

After, I shook hands with my professor and thanked him for the invite, apologized for my rags in the presence of so many riches, and grabbed my skateboard and headed off for a ride back to the motel I was staying at. Riding through the streets, about ten at night, I kept circling ideas of legacy, and our rubrics for measuring it.

Is everyone just waiting to make it?

To become the next big thing?

Are even the pastors of small churches drawn in by the dreams of celebrity?

The local traded in for only global?

I was at the conference, I was at the panel discussion, I had chats with the up-and-comers, and so much of it seemed like a kind of spirituality by platform. Maybe it was just me, but I felt the impulse to transpose it to my own life. Sure, I'd probably never share the spotlight, but I could put the same effort into my daily life. Multiply myself, build a legacy, and measure it with all the same stuff we measure all success by—being a box-office hit.

I got back to the room and saw my friends had gotten Shake Shack without me and we all sat on the plastic white chairs outside our second-floor room, overlooking the parking lot. The lights hummed; they were sterile, and bugs flew in their illumination. It was one of those patios that was also a walkway, lined by white iron balcony handrails. I asked them about the questions I was working through, and the answers were much the same as I had gotten from those at the event: less focused on vocational ministry but still legacy-framed by a kind of importance, success measured by status and spectators. It was the same old game. Save the world by emulating it.

Since then, I've seen shades of it, hints of it, just about everywhere I look. The myth of the ordinary Christian has all but disappeared. Everyone is looking to *be* something so that they can be someone. The Kingdom, it seems, is built on crowds; walks with God, no matter how local and homespun, depend upon admirers. Main Character Syndrome. It's the subconscious expectation that a life surrendered and devoted to Jesus will lead to recognition, acknowledgment, and accolades. And the converse is true: If there is no stage, if there's no rounds of applause, no future-proofing, how devoted could we really be?

But that's not how it works.

We're not the Main Character in this Story of Life. And that's an important lesson.

The Ordinary is the Miracle of Humanity.

We will all be forgotten, lost to the annals of time, swallowed up by the books of history. We want to be gods, even like God, pedestaled, and have our names *remembered*. But they won't be. And trust me, that's a good thing. We were designed to be ordinary, every day, destined by our finite frames. Here today, gone tomorrow.

We were not designed to be *mediocre*, that's not the same as ordinary; and we are not worthless, also not the same as ordinary. There is a Goodness in the ordinary routine of motherhood, of clocking into work, of sitting in traffic, of cleaning the house and paying the bills. A life of virtue, in the normalcy of life, is priceless, for it imbues that which is finite and temporal with the infinite and eternal. We do leave legacies, always, but what varies is *what* we pass on. It's that guiding whisper again, Steinbeck, helping me think soundly, helping me see clearly.

> You're going to pass something down no matter what you do or if you do nothing. Even if you let yourself go fallow, the weeds will grow and the brambles. Something will grow.[1]

And maybe instead of the flash, the noise, the pride, we can leave behind traces of the Hidden Music. We are ordinary, each of us, and we were Designed to be Good; to make God's Reality known in our local situations. Not simply "because the Bible tells us so." We do it as an act of war against the rebellion within ourselves and against the darkness that surrounds us. We do it as an embodiment of the Light, a way to push back the darkness, at the level that *truly* matters: the ordinary, every day expression of virtue rooted in Love. Goodness runs deeper than the extraordinary because it is founded upon that which is most Real.

There's this book I read, *The Beauty of Everyday Things*, by Soetsu Yanagi, a Japanese philosopher who founded the "folk craft" movement in Japan in the early 1900s. He wrote of the importance of *common* objects, things we use day in and day out, and how they shape our enjoyment and perception of the world. He said the machine-made, the mass-produced, creates nothing but the shallow and the cold, and how only the human hand can produce subtlety and warmth. There's a passage I need to share, at length, because it has put into words perfectly the need for Every Day Saints:

In recent times a shadow has fallen on our sense of beauty.... We no longer look upon objects as we used to, which is undoubtedly due to their poor quality. In the past, everyday objects were treated with care, with something verging on respect. While this attitude may, in part, have been a result of the scarcity of goods in past times, I believe it principally resulted from the honest quality of workmanship and the fact that the more an object was used, the more its beauty became apparent. As our constant companions in life, such objects gave birth to a feeling of intimacy and even affection.... When a person could point to what he was wearing and say, "This belonged to my grandfather," it was a source of pride. These days, however, the careless way things are made has robbed us of any feeling of respect or affection.[2]

And what if we acted like this for our whole lives? What if we recognized it was the personal, the embodied, the Real, that shapes us and forms us? What if we developed a sense of joy and gratitude in the *commonness* of life, in the beauty of all the every day things we do? What if we respected our bodies and souls? What if we saw the every day as beautiful? What if we were not robbed of the beauty of every day by some fleeting desire for recognition? What if we let, by our living, the infinite invade our finite spaces?

What if we became who we were intended to be?

The Every Day composes abiding legacy.

Chapter 26

Bodies Are Sacramental

IT'S THE PERFECT crime, the pursuit of celebrity. Behind that desire to be seen is the oldest sin of them all, pride. And when we're confronted with that pride, in any capacity, it's easy to brush it off as "service." Sure, the reality is that it's mostly self-serving, but it's easy to reframe pride as service to God, as in "I'm pointing others to Him." Ultimately, however, pride points to self; it demands to be seen, to be tended to, first and before all the rest. That's the skewed view of self and others, a contorted understanding of who we are as humanity. We are designed to be a reflection and a lens, to live a life that reveals God's virtue in the world. Pride destroys our ability to do that, to use our bodies to make the invisible, visible. Pride erases the true understanding of the person; it degrades the Beauty of the Ordinary.

I lived that degradation, lived in that erasure of the person. My drinking was selfish and prideful, ignorant of its effects on everyone else. My insecurity at "just" being a bike courier was the same—a blindness to the Beauty of Ordinary living. I wanted others to see *me*, to value *me*, to recognize *me* as some sort of superior man. I had missed the Hidden Music, the invitation to be a man of virtue, of Love expressed in every day life. To deliver not just food but a smile and joy. To make manifest Hidden and Eternal Realities.

After a few months at the climbing gym, I was decent enough to *project* certain climbs. All that means is a certain route would be too hard for me to be able to do in one gym session, but I could work at it, session after session, and eventually, who knows how many days or weeks later, I could get it. I was there on my own, shoes laced up, sipping at my coffee. They kept the heat low in the gym during the winter months, probably to save heating costs, but explained as mimicking what it's like to climb outside in the cold. I had been working on this climb for a few days already, learning where to place my hips to keep tight on the wall, mapping out where to hit the holds, and trying to nail my footwork. My hands were tiring and my toes were starting to hurt from pressing hard on tiny holds. When you hold something that tight, your muscles contract and you restrict blood flow, the muscles flex and expand, choking out every good thing a tiring body needs. Losing blood in the muscle bit by bit. Each failed attempt still required all my strength, the tightest grip I could muster, shoulders taut, back tense, reaching, slowly shifting weight. And I'd slip, lose a hand, or kick out a foot. I'd sit on the edge of the mat, looking out, breathing heavy, recovering. Sip at my coffee. Roll my wrists to get some blood moving again. It felt like my muscles would rip through my skin. A few people gathered around and were asking how it was going.

"I've been working at this the last few days," I say. "Trying to nail the last few moves."

"What are you thinking?" one asks, not wanting to spoil the problem.

I tell them my plan and say, "Essentially, I just need to be taller and stronger."

"Easier said than done."

And then I try again.

I'm working my way up the wall, feet secure, leaning and reaching for a hand. Shifting and stepping up. The few guys are watching me, they're saying, "You got this," and "Come on." And I'm slowly, methodically, moving through the part of the climb I know, getting to the part where I always fall. It's a big move, a bit taller of a reach, so I have to jump for it a bit, and I breathe in and hop for the hold. I hit it, but I can feel my grip slipping. The guys are yelling, and I get my feet back on the wall, shift in tight so I've got more hand on the hold, and then I've got it. A few moves later, I'm at the top. To the harmonious sounds of congratulations below.

I jump down and there's the customary fist bumps. I sit and breathe heavy. It wasn't much—a shared moment of something that I had been working on for a while—and at the same time, it was *much*. A lot is crammed into those local, real, embodied moments. The ones where instead of virtual applause we're met with the hands and shoulders of other bodies, the laughter and smiles of other humans. Real stuff.

This is the new vision for Life. It's local and residential; it's summed up in the personal, typified in the embodied. The Beauty of the Ordinary person is only *truly* and *deeply* experienced in that incarnated Reality of how we were designed—with bodies. We can't Love our neighbor as ourselves through the Mirror, Mirror. People need bodies; they need genuine Love. And then there is the Greatest Incarnational Reality: Jesus, God become man, showing us what it means to be fully human. The Incarnation, God embodied, is a revealing of the sacredness of the body, of its true purpose—to make visible the invisible, to make manifest all the Eternal Reality, to sing of the Hidden Music. The Architecture of Incarnation. Bodies are more than what they're made up of, bone and sinew; we are not just the sum of our parts. Bodies are sacramental, a symbol of the spiritual Reality:

> The body reveals the person. This phrase tells us all there is to know about the body. Science can examine our flesh in minute detail, down to our cells and even our DNA. But no amount of scientific exploration can replace the truth that our bodies reveal us, giving form to our innermost being and unique personality. Our bodies are sacramental—they make the invisible visible.[1]

We cannot stop the body from doing what the body does—revealing. Even when I was at my lowest, at Rock Bottom, my body revealed who I truly was, and my actions showed just how desperate and broken I had become. And your body does the same, if you just watch and listen. I didn't have eyes to see or ears to hear all the ways in which my body was urging me to stop, to become whole, to reorient itself toward the Source. My impulse toward drunkenness, my inclination toward apathy, my penchant for anger—they were all signposts that I was disordered, and as I gave in to each of those temptations, I continued to degrade and silence my body, and therefore I degraded and silenced my soul. Hence the question from the very beginning, *Why do you look for the living among the dead?* I was living a half-life.

We're told that success, that stardom, that platform and stage will satisfy us, that if we are seen and celebrated, we will be loved, that all the pain will go away. But the truth of it all is a lot different. The ratio of people who have existed to people who have been remembered in human history is heavily one-sided. The vast majority of us will fade away with the memories of those closest to us. Maybe one generation, maybe two or three, but eventually, all we are, and all we have been, will be dust. There's a paradox here, though, a seeming contradiction. When Jesus said that those who lose their lives find it,[2] I think He meant something like this: Those who live as they were designed to live, even though they lose everything, find Life.

The invitation is simple.

Cast off those self-serving yearnings of being remembered, of having pride tickled by every single eye that's on you. Forsake the lie of extraordinary, and return life to its proper place. Right in front of you. Beside you. All around you. Local. There are people you rub shoulders with at church, at the grocery store, on the bus, at work—everywhere—and each of them needs Real Love. They don't need a celebrity; they need you, and they need me. Each of us has a local context, a world that we exist in, move in, have all our being in, and in that context, in those varied situations, is where everything that matters happens.

The invitation is to use *place*, to use where we exist in a family, a church, a job, a school—everything—and to know that through you God intends to reveal Himself, to make the invisible visible. To change the world, to change ourselves, requires real work and real people; we cannot rely on an internet guru, a church program, or even status to change the world. Once we start thinking that way—that money, sex, and power; the lust of the eyes, the lust of the flesh, the pride of life, are the tools of renewal and transformation—we start trying to cure the disease with the poisons that got us all in this mess to begin with. The reality is that most revivals take place in the secret places, local and intimate.

Bodies enact ceremonies which Guide our Loves.

Chapter 27

Liturgies for Local Living

THERE WERE SOME nights in England that were strangely reminiscent of days gone by in Toronto, almost like living a déjà vu, nights where I'd go for a walk by myself, and head to a pub for a drink, and have a smoke in a park. And while they were similar, they felt different, and not just because I was in England. It was like I had come full circle, but somehow, also gone deeper. I had a few cigarettes in my coat pocket and lit one up as I left our flat. I walked south, down the streetlight-lit road, toward the botanical gardens, trying to retrace my pilgrimage so far—where I had started, and how I got to where I am. Hindsight, so they say, is twenty-twenty.

I was still asking questions about my identity, but I wasn't the same guy knocking at a door with a few sushi platters, trying to tell the person I'm delivering to that I used to work as a project manager. I didn't care anymore. My questions now were about Sainthood, learning to *be* who God had intended me to be, not pretending to be anybody else. Not forcing it, not playing the part I was supposed to, but simply beginning to exist as designed.

It's early evening, and I'm sitting near the fountains in the local gardens, and people are walking by, talking, enjoying their evening. *I know the answers*, I'm thinking to myself as I drag on my smoke. But that's not going to cut it anymore. Religion is a practice. Belief is part of the whole, but it is not the whole. Embodiment is the whole.

Winter had mostly set in, but it wasn't as cold as Canada, so I knew I had a bit of time before I familiarized myself with a booth near a fireplace at a local pub. The fountain is trickling, water falling from each tier, back down to the reservoir—a localized water cycle. Light from steel lamps is catching the droplets as they drip and it's highlighting the cascading ripples. I had to let go, I had to surrender. A kind of relinquishing, the giving up of all the things I had used to keep me in control of my life. I had to leave the small little prison I had made for myself—crafted out of insecurity and shame and fear and cowardice, out of drunkenness and anger and apathy—and I needed to set out into a brave new world, one where I didn't know everything, out into the unknown—where what matters most wasn't just what I've studied but how I actually lived.

I stomp out my cigarette and start the walk over to The Stag's Head. I was having conversations in my mind, some with myself, some with the people who had shared disdain with all the ways I had failed, but most of the conversations were with pretend people. Made-up. Suited to my needs. You know the kind I'm talking about. I'm trying to explain to them, to myself, that this whole thing is going to take time. My life was under development, and so far, all I had done was tear it all down. The rebuilding needed to take time and intentionality. And that was okay. It takes all of us time, in between everything else in life. Like I said, there is no special reprieve for existential dilemmas, and the same is true for the becoming. Except for one thing: You don't need reprieve; you don't need to put life on hold. Becoming a Saint happens right in the middle of everything. Becoming a Saint is woven into the fabric of every day life, if you use it right. It just takes time.

People have their collars flipped up against the winter's wind, but they're still nodding as we pass by each other on the sidewalk. I'm still talking to myself and someone asks me for a light—startling me up out of my dreamworld. I pull out my lighter and thumb the ignition; sparks mix with butane and a flame is born. He inhales, says thanks, and heads off, smoke rising and disappearing on the breeze. The lights are on in the shops as I walk past, bright orange against the stone-cold blue of the street; the cobblers wave—they had resoled my leather boots the week before.

It's almost impossible to change an outlook. I'm talking to some imaginary person in my mind still as I stroll down the street. *We cannot be reasoned out of something we were never reasoned into.* We were born into a worldview, and we were taught it, shown it, by our tradition and context. No one argued us into our positions for living; we slowly adopted them by degrees, day by day, and with each passing moment. My hands are in my pockets, thumbing the lighter, still using these imaginary conversations as a way to process. My shoulders are shrugged, helping to keep the bite of the wind off my neck, and I know that there isn't enough information in the world, not enough arguments or syllogisms, that will be able to give me new eyes to see. And I figure I'm not alone in this; I'm not that special or unique. I don't see much of my surroundings, I'm too lost in the conversation in my mind, each step made by routine, because I had walked this path some hundred times.

You and I require a full and healthy apologetic. Truth and Reason form only part of the whole—and that *part* is not enough for the kind of transformation, the kind of personal revolution, we need. We need a view that swallows up the entire person, one that demands everything from all of who we are.

There was this shortcut, the Frog Walk, that went along the old cemetery and popped back up near the pub. It's lined with trees, and the walkway is narrow. The evening blues are deepening into a thick charcoal, and the wind is cut off by the drooping branches and stubborn leaves. *Life takes time*, whispered or mouthed, but not just in my mind. A Good Life doesn't come easy; I need to become, I need to embrace and retrain. I had all this impetus, the old stuff, that I needed to shake off. Trying the same thing over and over, expecting different results. The mark of insanity. I had to embrace the time it took to embody the virtues—the means by which we all head Saintward.

It's up this flight of stairs, then out to a roundabout, and down

Psalter Lane to The Stag's Head. I order a pint of my friend's favorite, leave a few pounds on the bar, and grab a seat near the fire.

This could be my whole life, I'm thinking.

A night at the pub, a late dinner with my wife, a church community, some deep friendships, a climbing gym. It was small, but it was precious. I didn't need a title, I didn't need a red carpet, I didn't need bright lights, and I didn't need thousands of eyes. I didn't need to be someone to some horde of people, I could just be *me*. And that *me* could be loved by a bunch of other real *me*s who I did all my life with. I could be local, like the fountain's water cycle. I could be here today and gone tomorrow, like that man's cigarette smoke. It's all borrowed time anyway; why not spend it on that which matters most? I would be forgotten, but I would be Good. I would be remembered, with a smile, by Grace, by my wife, by my family and my friends, by those whose lives I mingled with. And we'd all disappear together, just like a smile does, with a breath.

And again, I'm thinking about the substance of the life of Jesus. Of His ordinary way of being. The fireplace pops and crackles and its warmth radiates over my cold body. I'm thinking about the thirty silent years, the time so *unremarkable* we don't know anything about it, but it's the time that shaped Him. I'm thinking about the *how* of Jesus' maturing, and then about His teachings from the mountainside, and the meals He shared together with every manner of person. I'm thinking about the long and dusty walks with His friends from town to town. I'm thinking about how often He went out of His way to *really* meet someone for who they were, and to show them an unconditional love that would set them free. How His entire mission was to be about His Father's work—and that work was Love.

I could do that, I'm thinking to myself, looking out at everyone else in the pub, seeing their smiles, imagining that their lives are just as full and alive as mine. *I could commit to the way of unconditional Love, of revealing, with my local and embodied life, Jesus.* And it's more than that too. It's dawning on me, radiating through me, like that fireplace that warmed the chill out of my bones, that my pursuit of Jesus was the pursuit of the Hidden Music; He was the Source. He is the Giver of Life, and as we follow Him, we are drawn up into that Life by an embodied participation.

How had I missed this?

How had I missed this one answer that tied everything together, that drew all things to itself?

I'm sitting there, trying to take it all in, and I'm smiling, almost laughing, mostly at myself. At my childishness, about my rage—like tantrums—at how little I knew, but how much I thought I had figured out. About how it all slipped by me, right under my nose. The "forest for the trees" kind of thing.

I had come full circle.

Almost back to where I began. "I am the man who with the utmost daring discovered what had been discovered before."[1] This was no grand invention, not anything new, not anything state-of-the-art. Any impulse I had to find a new way, to be ahead of the curve, to unearth some secret knowledge—all of it—just proved how backward I was. I left my small prison and stepped out into the great expanse; but that expanse is not unknown, not an abyss. It is well-lived-in. I was just the man in the cave, wishing there was more than flickering shadows on the wall. And in leaving I found something very ancient, something very alive, and something very lived in. I was trying to find some new way, and all I found were old footsteps, well-worn paths, reeds pressed down into hard soil. Chesterton speaks to me again, from a remembering, his voice echoing through pages I had read:

> I did try to found a heresy of my own; and when I had put the last touches to it, I discovered that it was orthodoxy.[2]

Turning the pint glass in my hand, watching the last few golden ounces bubbling up into the foamy head. I take a sip, letting everything—the fireplace, the pint, and the idea that my life could be consumed by a Living Love, Jesus—wash over me.

I didn't have it figured out then, but I do now. This is a *cosmic* piety, a universal devotion. A kind of *being* that exists *under* the Divine Reality. Maximos the Confessor, a monk and theologian born in the sixth century, proposed the idea of the "Cosmic Christ"—that everything in all of Creation finds its Source in the Person of Jesus. And that is where we find ourselves, born from and destined back into Jesus, the Author of Life. Like I said, reason isn't going to get you there, and it's not going to change a lived history; what we need is for our hearts to be captured, to be set ablaze, to be engrossed in the True Reality—to hear the Hidden Music.

Beauty is the apologetic needed, primarily, not Truth. Beauty is antecedent, it comes before; we are struck by it and enraptured by it, and it attracts us, beckons to us, that we might "be united with the beauty we see, to pass into it, to receive it into ourselves, to bathe in it, to become part of it."[3] That's what we need to wake up within ourselves: an inconsolable longing that drives us further up and further in. Beauty steals our hearts and orients them toward the Cosmic Christ; it drowns us and overwhelms us; we are defenseless against a beautiful poem, a work of art, a moving film, a dance—it gets right at our cores, swells up our souls so that our bodies buckle, about to burst at the seams. That's what changes us, what reorients broken and defective outlooks; we cannot be reasoned out of that which we were not reasoned into, but we can fall in Love again. We can behold, and so be transformed. My version of Christianity paled in comparison to the Real thing, which is God's Reality.

I'm putting my coat back on, taking my pint glass up to the oak bar, and saying goodbye to the bartender, and walking through the wooden doors. Out into the cold night, dark and bracing, but with a kind of warmth in my chest. Like carrying the fireplace with me, except this time it's the Light of Jesus. I light another cigarette, and I'm thinking this is one of my liturgies, a way to use my body for contemplation. And when I inhale the warm aroma, I'm thinking that my thoughts are mostly prayers, and that they rise, like a kind of incense, to God.

The cold doesn't nip at me quite the same way, and the sharp air feels refreshing. As I walk under streetlights, I can see my shadow circle me and then disappear on the dark pavement, over and over, and I'm reflecting on the Great Commandment:

"Teacher, which *is* the greatest commandment in the law?"

Jesus said to him, "'You shall love the Lord your God with all your heart, with all your soul, and with all your mind.' This is *the* first and great commandment. And *the second is* like it: 'You shall love your neighbor as yourself.' On these two commandments hang all the Law and the Prophets."[4]

There was something about me—my life, my ears, my eyes—that had impaired my being able to understand the vast simplicity of the Way of Jesus. To be drawn into the Source of Love, and then make manifest that Love. Most of what I needed to do now was to unplug my ears and uncover my eyes. That was the new way, but it was as old as time itself.

That's what all of us need to do: Uncover our eyes. And that takes time. In some ways, I could have just told you this, but that would go against everything I'm *actually* saying. This uncovering takes time and is embodied. Knowing the line, the facts, won't drop the scales. You need to embark on your own journey of becoming a Saint. You need to have the warmth of Jesus radiate and thaw every cold and frozen bit of your life. Have His light shine on you, the same way it did for me, even in a drunken stupor at the Bottom of life. The struggle, the path, has always been embodied.

You might not have a drinking problem; you might not want to end it all; you might not quit your job; you might not have those haunted, sleepless nights; and maybe you won't weep in front of Raymond; and you might not run away to England—but you do have demons of your own. You have all kinds of coping mechanisms, ways for dealing with all the anguish of life, ones that you hope will answer all the misery of your mediocrity. But they won't. They will lead you to the pit, just like they led me there.

And there is only one answer.

I'm getting home, making the last turn up the laneway, heading up the stone stairs to our second-floor flat, and I'm feeling the invitation. Embrace the Cosmic Christ. My Life is the sacrament, given by Jesus as a means of Divine Grace to be a sign and symbol of His True Reality. Stab me and I'd bleed the Life to come, look into my eyes and you'd see a glimmer of Hope, hold my hand and you'd feel something of eternity.

Maybe not now, maybe not yet, but one day. Shadows, sure, but running toward the Substance.

I unlock the door and walk through. Home.

Beauty is the apologetic.

A LITURGY OF INCARNATION

Surrender, by listening, to the Way of God.

The full person, body and soul, is an offering; obedience is momentum.

Embodied Love is the path into all Virtue.

Recapture the Beauty of Becoming.

The Ordinary is Holy.

The Every Day composes abiding legacy.

Bodies enact ceremonies which Guide our Loves.

Beauty is the apologetic.

Act IV.
The Symphony of Embodiment

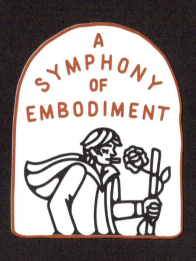

Chapter 28

A Study in Desire

GRACE WAITS FOR us, even at the Bottom.

No expectations, no judgment, just the kind of compassion that rushes out to meet us, to throw arms around us, to bring us home. That was my story, I think, looking back. The one where the Prodigal relents, gives up, and returns to the Father. I had all these conjured images of prodigals: of tattered robes, disheveled hair, emaciated faces—the classic image of the broken ones returning home. What I couldn't see was all the ways I was a prodigal: the shined shoes, the tailored pants, the branded button-downs, the smile—all just a mask for the brokenness underneath. Whitewashed tombs. Thinking there was no need of any healing because I didn't *look* sick on the outside.

The boring catastrophe.

Then there was my *old* way of trying to fix it: follow the rules, do the stuff, and drink myself ragged whenever things didn't seem to line up. The Prodigal was at the Feast of Pigs and I judged him from the bottom of a bottle. He and I were much the same, however. And that's a bitter pill to swallow; we judge those to whom we are all too similar; they are mirrors that reflect back to us all our weaknesses. And even there, from the bottom of the bottle, Grace was waiting for me; Jesus was singing the Hidden Music, inviting me into His Life. I thought my way up was to find Him, but He had been there, at the Bottom, all along; I was just blind. So blind. And that's generally our problem: the blindness—we have it backward. We think we're responsible for the first step, but that has already been made. All our effort boils down to this:

Receive, be filled, and overflow.

> The question is not "How am I to find God?" but "How am I to let myself be found by him?" The question is not "How am I to know God?" but "How am I to let myself be known by God?" And, finally, the question is not "How am I to love God?" but "How am I to let myself be loved by God?" God is looking into the distance for me, trying to find me, and longing to bring me home.[1]

It's late morning, Aislinn is teaching English online, and I'm grabbing a backpack and heading out to get some groceries for us. There's some drying and dying leaves at our entryway, the last few from the trees finally giving in to winter's cold, and they crunch under my boots. My time alone now feels different. I don't feel lonely. Before these epiphanies, if I can call them that, before embracing the way of the Saint, alone felt like being on the outside, separated from Reality. Now, alone feels different. It feels like solitude, a place for undivided attention, a time for prayer. These walks, down the same old lanes, feel like recited prayers, just for my body.

You've heard me say it a few times, but hindsight is twenty-twenty, and there was this situation, a conversation, that popped into my mind as I shopped for ground beef and onions, for peppers and celery and carrots. One that didn't fully make sense when it happened, but one I could reinterpret in light of everything I had come to see.

It was during that time when I was questioning if God really loved me, and if I could know it, not just in my head but in my whole self. I had been talking with someone, and we were circling the whole topic—probably my fear of being rejected or misunderstood. But eventually the Band-Aid had to be ripped off.

"I just don't know if God loves *me*," I'd said.

"Of course He does," came the reply. "You know that."

"I don't. I know all *about* it, but I don't know it. It's like I'm just a tourist, visiting the sites, doing the things I'm supposed to—taking a few pictures to commemorate the occasion—but then I just move on—"

There was no pause before the reply—no moment to consider, to genuinely respond—just the typical six-shooter of platitudes locked and loaded, finger on the trigger: "God Loves you; that's all there is to it." And then came the inevitable. "'God demonstrates His own love toward us, in that while we were still sinners, Christ died for us.'" A verse to save me.

Done and dusted, at least in his mind.

The conversation had droned on, saying much yet getting nowhere. And now I know it's because we were speaking different languages, we were missing each other on what it means to *know*. The difference of knowing by explanation versus by experience. I'd thought I had to find Love, rather than be found by it. And now I know that my longing wasn't a one-way street, it wasn't just a Lost Son seeking out his Father. No, God had been inviting me back to Himself all along. He wanted me to *know* Him.

I'm putting the last few groceries in my basket, grabbing a chocolate bar for Ais, and getting in line. *Now I know*, I'm thinking, *that everything, even back then, and even back in Toronto, was an invitation—I'd just been blind to it.* Jesus had always been singing the Hidden Music; He's the Source, the fountainhead from which cascades all Goodness, Truth, and Beauty. Every moment is an invitation, a summoning. It was a survival mode that gave me tunnel vision, only able to see half the picture.

The lady behind the register is ringing up the cabbage, the beans, the tomato sauce, and we smile at each other. I had been left unsatisfied in my life because I was looking for *this* life to satisfy—putting *too* much on everything around me, attempting to fashion it into something that could sustain and hold up *all* my needs and desires and

A Study in Desire

wants and worship. I hand her the money, get the change, and put all the ingredients for tonight's chili in my backpack. *And when nothing could sustain me,* I'm thinking as I walk home, *when everything was crushed under the weight of my need, rage followed.* The vicious cycle repeated until I learned that *all* those longings and all their corresponding pleasures were not the *telos*—the end, the goal. They were signposts fashioned and formed to point my whole self toward the Source. Another guide whispers in my mind:

> If I find in myself a desire which no experience in this world can satisfy, the most probable explanation is that I was made for another world. If none of my earthy pleasures satisfy it, that does not prove that the universe is a fraud. Probably earthly pleasures were never meant to satisfy it, but only to arouse it, to suggest the real thing.[2]

That was Lewis again, reminding me that half measures won't do. A few years later I discovered that Peter Kreeft had taken this passage from Lewis and formalized it, calling it the "Argument From Desire," and his syllogism goes like this:

> **Premise 1**: Every natural, innate desire in us corresponds to some real object that can satisfy that desire.
> **Premise 2**: But there exists in us a desire which nothing in time, nothing on earth, no creature can satisfy.
> **Conclusion**: Therefore there must exist something more than time, earth and creatures, which can satisfy this desire.
> This something is what people call "God" and "life with God forever."[3]

I was looking for the *Something More*; we all are, and we're trying to turn sex and drink and success and relationships and pleasure and everything else *into* that Something More, but every time, they collapse under the weight of our infinite longing. Structurally unsound for the load of our need. We need to allow those longings space, give them some room to breathe, not try to silence and numb them with every kind of distraction and idol.

All along, from beginning until now, I was searching for God—not in some cliché catchphrase sense, not like a fortune cookie or bumper sticker, not a secret phrase, not in the whole *the obstacle is the way*, but in the sense that He was behind it all. I wanted Him, and settled for so much less. He is the Source of all the Beauty I longed for, the Author of Goodness, the Genesis of all that which is True. He sings the Hidden Music; He beckons to us all, calling us *up* rather than *out*. That's the Real Christian view: that God made everything Good, and everything, as it reflects Him, reflects aspects of that Goodness; everything that is Beautiful finds its fulfillment in Him, and so, too, for Love and Truth.

The soul's desire can only be satisfied by the Infinite Jesus.

Chapter 29

Longings Fulfilled

WHEN I SAY God was after me, I mean it—every leaf, every story, every song; He was after me when I was drunk at five thirty in the morning, shaking me awake. He was there in Aislinn's kind eyes, loving me through my darkest moments. He was there behind Raymond's patience as I wept out a reclusive fury. He was there in the open house of my friend's aunt and uncle, and He was there in the peace of that prayer meeting and in the pints that drew us in. He was there in the words of my friends Ben and Jon, and He was there, listening and speaking, as I walked the city streets, smoking and praying, and heard all the voices of past Saints: Lewis and Chesterton and Dostoevsky, Saint Gregory, and everyone else. And He will be there for you too. I just want you to be able to see it faster than I did, to hear His voice and follow His call. You do not need to hit Rock Bottom. Learn from my mistakes.

All of these, though, as good as they were, are just shades of God's True Reality. And in them, and through them, God summons all people to Himself—to long for *more* Goodness, *more* Truth, and *more* Beauty. These shades could not bear up all I longed for; the gifts cannot replace the Giver. I needed the Substance; I desired the Source. I longed not for *what* the cosmos was made of but for the *Who*—the Wellspring of Life.

What we need, collectively, is to learn how God expresses Himself.

To hear Him on His own terms, not those we tend to force upon Him, not the ones given to us, and not the ones we have fabricated in all our hurts and confusions and doubts. The Cosmic View is an invitation *into*; to begin to inhabit a world that will reshape us—like stepping into a new story, into a world, like Middle-earth, that overwhelms and envelops us. One where we are small but not insignificant.

It's about embracing a new mythology, a new way of Life. It's a childlike belief that will lead us deeper into the wild adventure of virtue. I never thought whether orcs, for example, were *true* when I first read *The Lord of the Rings* because I knew them to be *true*—true as part of that world, and true in every symbolic sense. I didn't doubt the elves or dwarves, I never doubted that the Undying Lands lay just beyond the sea. It was all true. It all sang to my soul. That's what my Christianity started to become—not a need for cold hard proofs but as the place of longings fulfilled.[1] A *world* that evoked wonder and awe. An invitation into a Cosmic Piety. A Bright Shadow that swallowed me whole.

Part of the *how* was learning to experience and see God in and through those Transcendentals: Goodness, Truth, and Beauty. This is the language for a new land. If every act of God is Love, then everything He does is an expression of that Love. And to experience who He is, we must follow His Goodness, His Truth, and His Beauty.

There was this time I remember, when I was twelve, that my body felt the force of virtue. Felt like it was bigger than to-do lists, felt like it was calling to me, exhorting me, demanding more. It was my friend's birthday, and our little trio—Stephen, Josh, and me—went to the movies. His dad took us to see *Gladiator*. We're in the theater, the three of us with his dad, popcorn on our laps, the preshow running on repeat. The three of us can't stop talking, and everyone there is the same; the room pulsed—each laugh, popcorn eaten by the handful, the leaning in and checking watches for start times—everything just kept building. And the lights dimmed, and we all fell in line.

Silent.

There's a hand on-screen, wedding ring, gauntlet on the arm, the fingers hovering over a field of wheat as the man walks. The scene cuts to a Roman general, wolf pelt on his shoulders, and he's looking over a battle-torn land, turning, walking through his ranks, his men kneeling in smiling reverence as he passes. He stops, talks with someone, waiting to get intelligence, waiting for the return of a scout; too much time has passed. Scene cuts to a whinnying horse, a man riding it through the burnt land toward the general and his army. The rider is met by a fellow soldier and there's blood on the horse's neck. The scene cuts again: A bearded man, holding an axe in one hand and a head in the other, steps atop a felled tree, and he yells something in a foreign tongue. And it's echoed by a mass of warriors emerging from the white, barren forest behind him. He yells again, holding up the head of the scout, throwing it as a warning to the opposing Roman force. Scene cut. The general kneels. He grabs some muddy earth, smells it, and rubs it in his hands. He stands. "Strength and honor," he says and mounts his horse.

"At my signal," he says, looking over the battlefield, "unleash hell."[2]

I was entranced.

I didn't know movies could *do* that, could *be* that. It played on for the next two and a half hours and it changed me. I watched something: the tale of a man bound by honor, by virtue, who endured all manner of affliction and remained *good*. The kind of valor that fills your heart to the point of bursting; the kind that urges you to follow, to join in, to abide by the same code. To stand bravely against the storm. To embody strength and honor. "Courage is not simply one of the virtues, but the form of every virtue at the testing point."[3]

These scenes are on replay in my mind often, like the same loop as the movie's preshow. I'm considering, almost always, that it takes courage to *be* Good. And giving in is a cowardice I was all too familiar with. God is the Source of the Good, and from Him flows all manner of Goodness. Goodness is *about* virtue. The virtues—humility, charity, gratitude, temperance, chastity, patience, and diligence—are the framework for what constitutes a Good person. If a person is Good, the philosophers and theologians say, they're going to embody these virtues, rather than their opposites.

There's more to this, though, than the external manifestation of the virtues. Mere obligation, or duty, is not enough. The intention to participate in the Good, a unity and cooperation with God. Not out of duty but in Love. The Christian ethic is one of Love, and from that Love, that union, that relationship, flows every Good act. Virtue is an inside-out kind of thing, starting with the same sort of *entrancement* I felt watching a Roman general stand for the Good, and longing to *be* the same.

Jesus, on a hillside, the Sea of Galilee below Him, started to speak of those who are *blessed*. He was speaking to the poor, the mistreated, the sorrowful, the broken, the outsiders, the oppressed, the seekers, and He's offering them an invitation to participate in Goodness. He saw this crowd, their pain, their confusion, their desire to find liberation, and He offered them revolution; not with respect to violence but a revolution of Love and Goodness. He validated their pains and their yearnings, and He pointed them toward that which will satisfy: Himself. His Way. The Way of the Kingdom—to *do* only that which the Father is doing.

Goodness, as a Transcendental, is an expression of who God is. The invitation for all of us is to *enjoy* who God is by participating in that Goodness, by using our whole Life to display that Goodness to the world around us. That way lies Sainthood. Using every moment as an opportunity to conform ourselves to God, to stand bravely against everything that would oppose the life of virtue. That leads us further into Jesus, who is the Author of Life. Every other path leads away from Him; Rock Bottom is just a stop along the way. Departing from Life has the consequence of unmaking us, dis-integrating us, until we cease to *be* at all.

Virtue, Goodness, is the practice of participating in God's Love.

Chapter 30

Truth Is Not Mere Fact

THERE WAS ANOTHER couple who took us under their wing while we were in England. We had landed there in early September, which meant we were away from home during Thanksgiving, Christmas, and New Year's, and not only did they open their home to us during those times, they also had us over for dinner often. Their generosity was another medicine that kept homesickness at bay. A bit of Hidden Music.

We're at their place one evening, the four of us seated in the living room, waiting for dinner to be ready, getting to know each other, sharing stories. Just the lamps are on and there's some olives and nuts and cheese on the coffee table. They're asking us the *real* why behind coming to England. At that point, all they had heard was some Canadian friends were joining the church for a while. So we shared with them all my *stuff*, and all my questions, and how I was looking to live life, normally, in a space where I had the freedom to learn.

"That doesn't quite make rational sense," Chris says. That's his name. "But it does make a lot of sense spiritually."

"What do you mean?" I ask.

"Well," he says, and sips at his gin and tonic, "there's lots of things that don't make any sense, rationally speaking, when it comes to following Jesus. 'Sell all your possessions and follow me,' for example. But Jesus is after something more than rational; He is after the Truth."

And that put so much of my life into sharp focus.

"Rationally speaking," Ann says, that's her name, "it didn't make sense for Jesus to die. At least, humanly speaking. Think of how all His followers reacted—hiding away, deep sorrow. But spiritually? He knew His Death would be the Gateway to Life."

And more comes into focus.

The oven timer goes off, and we take our seats at the kitchen table, a Thai curry spooned out into bowls, grace for the meal, and Aislinn asks them to explain that difference, between human rationality and Divine wisdom, a bit more.

"Truth can't be reduced to facts," Ann says. "Truth is a Person."

"And knowing the Truth isn't about acquiring facts," Chris says. "It's about knowing the Person."

We spend the rest of the night on a lot less heavy subjects, talking about making mischief as kids, sharing jokes, and then hugs as we leave. But that night, that brief conversation, was a perspective change for me—a revelation that we don't acquire Truth. We participate in it, we partake in it, not simply mentally but relationally. Truth is about a unity and harmony with Jesus, about how God views and understands the world.

This is more than our human finiteness compared with God's infinity; and it's more than God simply knowing all the facts that we haven't quite mastered yet. This isn't computational; that just reduces Jesus to a supercomputer—omniscient by operating system. This is more about a state of being, an ontology. Jesus is Truth. Truth *before* everything we can see and touch and measure existed; Truth on which every other thing depends. A Living Truth whose Divine Imprint marks everything in the Cosmos. Everything coheres, makes sense, can be understood because it finds its source in Jesus.

Being finite means we have to learn to interpret reality; it's why what Chris and Ann said makes so much sense. We try to interpret our lives rationally, make sense of the breakups, the cancer diagnosis, the job loss, the rejections, all of it, from our perspective. We interpret the facts, we try to draw meaning out of it, and then make some plan, something that will get us through. But that's not what comes first. Truth is a Person: Jesus. And, count our lucky stars, He's given us an interpretation of His Person—found primarily in the Gospels. We can know the Truth, know Jesus, by His actions.[1] The infinite and unknowable makes Himself known to us, embodied. Or as Saint John said it:

> And the Word became flesh and dwelt among us, and we beheld His glory, the glory as of the only begotten of the Father, full of grace and truth.[2]

Jesus said that if we have seen Him, we've seen the Father.[3] Jesus makes the invisible visible, the incomprehensible comprehensible. And I hope you're catching that our call is to do the same, to use our bodies and reveal our souls. Jesus does the same thing: uses His body to reveal His nature, that is, God's nature.

We took a taxi home from Chris and Ann's place, and when we got to our flat and got ready for bed, Ais and I were talking about what it means for Truth to be a Person, to experience Jesus by participation.

"It's sort of like being in love," Aislinn says. "It's about being in harmony with each other, united. Being in love, staying in love, is the commitment to remain *together*."

And now that makes more sense than ever.

For us, seeking to live in the Truth, to participate in Jesus, who is the Source of all Truth, we need to be in Harmony with Him. To hear the Hidden Music, and tune ourselves to its melody. It's an abiding; and from that abiding flows every other True thing—theology, philosophy, science, art, music—all in accord, a universe flawlessly expressing the sacred signature of its Maker.

Jesus is the lens for interpreting the Cosmos; understanding comes by intimacy.

Chapter 31

Rivers Run with Wine

YOU CAN STAY just about anywhere in Europe for at least three months, no questions asked, if you're Canadian. In England, it's 180 days. No visa applications, just hop on the flight, have a place to stay, get your stamp, and move on. That's how we stayed in England for six months and it's how we took our trip to Ireland. Our plan, since the first week of landing in jolly ole England, had always been to head to the Emerald Isle. In late November we caught a short flight from Manchester to Dublin with just our backpacks, our hiking boots, and a few places to stay. Aislinn had couch surfed before on a backpacking trip a few years previous, so we opted for the same thing. You can sign up on a website, and people offer up their couches, or spare rooms, or blow-up mattresses for all kinds of travelers. The cost is connection, which sounds trite, but it's a beautiful way to experience a place.

Our plan was to land in Dublin, explore the city, and then meet our first host—a Polish guy who had moved to Ireland for work. We spent the night eating pierogies and drinking a homemade spiced rum; he told us of his old loves and about his trips to Spain and how he wants as many people to enjoy what travel does to a person as possible. He tells us to come back anytime.

The next morning he's gone by the time we're awake, and we're packing up and prepping for the next leg of our road trip around the south of the island. His house still smells a bit like pierogies, and it's decorated in folk art and glass statues. We're making some coffees for the road, and you can hear it dripping into the pot as we roll up our sweaters and tuck them into our backpacks.

By day's end we need to be in Kilkenny, but we've got a hike to do on the way, in Glendalough. The sky is a muted cerulean and the first part of the hike is through a marsh on a boardwalk. Everything feels alive by a kind of diversity—the rusted gold of the heather to the pale blue of the sky, the amber boardwalk, the cream brush, the jades and bronze of cattails. Then it's around a lake. Quiet, stone graves mark the entryway, and up through a mossy wood toward an abandoned mining village.

Waterdrops bead on our jackets, the wind calls the brush and branches to dance, our noses redden from cold. The mining village is at the base of a mountain, and there are piles of stones—some in circles, some in the shapes of long-gone buildings, some looking like filled-in tunnels. We pass through, up the steep incline, gravel crushed and rolling under our boots, our legs braced with each step up. A fog settles in, and the sun is trying to burn through; and all it's doing is highlighting floating thistle seeds.

Near the summit there's a thunder—a mountain river—and there's a herd of deer drinking. The brush is thick here, and it's that same burning-rust color, alive against the cobalt sky and frothing river, against the golden fleece and hazel antlers of the stag. Beauty by contrast. They follow us after we cross a wooden bridge; floating, illuminated thistle seeds dancing all around us. It's silent up there, just the gentle whispers of a dancing meadow and the staccato snaps of brush beneath the deer. From up here we can see the lake, we can see the marsh, we can see the old church and graveyard we parked at, and we can see the pub our little hike ends at.

There's this trail that goes down through the woods, ragged stones placed flat-edge up as makeshift stairs. The trees are saturated, vibrant by the fog and damp, and drops of water drip off leaves. The cold is on us, under our skin, in the nooks and crannies of our bones, telling us that we have to sit by a fire, have a drink, have a meal. So we oblige.

The pub is brick inside, cathedral-style ceiling, giant truss beams, planks laid over them, and every inch is covered in art and framed vintage advertisements. We're seated at a small table near the bar, and we order some chips and some stews, and my first pint of Guinness in Ireland. We're waiting for the food, and our hands are tingling back awake from the cold. And then it comes, the pint glass, filled with the Irish champagne. I was told by so many people that any pint of it I've had in Canada would not, could not, compare to having it straight from the source. There's the creamy, foamy head, the molasses stout proudly settling below, the side of the pint glass stamped with the white and gold lettering, a pearl of condensation tracing down the curve of it. Violin plays through some speakers somewhere, and it feels like the chandelier we're sitting under is a spotlight: my moment on center stage. The glass is cold to the touch and sloshes as I pick it up to my mouth; it's rich, creamy, like a chocolate dark-roasted espresso. There's a foam mustache on my lip, droplets on my stubble, and the stout warms me from the inside out.

Aislinn asks, "What do you think?"

And all I can do is smile.

I had been talking about that first draught for a few weeks, and now it was a moment fulfilled. This was another tune of the Hidden Music. And these are the moments that shape the life of a Saint, of participation in Beauty. It doesn't need to be a Guinness in an Irish pub, but it does need to stir you, to inspire you, and welcome you into the Life to come. And maybe that sounds too small, too trite. How much can all that really change? And it's impossible to measure—but it's a contrast. I had spent so much of my life participating in the liturgies of Death—of rage and disillusion, of apathy and disenchantment, of bitterness and discontent—and they almost killed me. There's no knowing just how much Good comes from the opposite, from participating in Beauty, day in and day out.

"This place is magic," Aislinn says. "No one was lying when they told us that." And she's right—everything seems awake, almost animate, like if you leaned hard enough on the bar it would start telling you all the secrets it has overheard; like if you stared too long at a painting, it'd wink at you; like when you opened the door to leave, you might just end up in Valinor.

It's hard to imagine, at least for me, Ireland any other way.

When we were driving out that night, farther south to Kilkenny, listening to jazz on our phones, we start talking about *just* how beautiful this place is, about how its mythos fills the atmosphere. And sometimes it takes the obvious for us to see the Hidden. Chesterton taught me that:

> [Fairy] tales say that apples were golden only to refresh the forgotten moment when we found that they were green. They make rivers run with wine only to make us remember, for one wild moment, that they run with water.[1]

And that's what Ireland was for me: a remembering of the beauty of everyday things. I didn't need idyllic mountain hikes every day, guided by stags and glowing thistle seeds. What I needed was eyes to see—to see the Beauty, God's Beauty, all around me. Maybe I needed to picture my bed as made of clouds, so I could remember, for a moment, the warm embrace of a good night's sleep. Maybe I needed to imagine my dinners with friends as feasts of ambrosia, the food of the gods, so I could remember how nourishing a meal together is. Maybe I needed to remember, by imagination and through Beauty, just how Big the world is. Maybe we all need it.

The world is Big and the world is Wonderful because of who has made it: Jesus. Beauty is objective and from that objectivity we have these subjective experiences and enjoyments of it. Jesus is the Source of Beauty, and He expresses it with infinite creativity. Beauty carries within it all mythos and lore we can imagine because in Him is all Beauty, infinite and inexpressible. All of the tales, the songs, the legends; all of the statues and art galleries; the joy of laughing around a table, of going on long walks by the lake, of a hand to hold, of a bed to rest in, the smile of a child; they are all pointing, proclaiming the Beauty of Jesus.

The world is not just systems and formulas, not just machine, not simply functional. The world is Beautiful by design, and every bit of that Beauty finds its source in the Master Artist who crafted our cosmos. And that's why all this Beauty beckons to us, bids us further up, bids us further in. That's why we cannot be satisfied, it's why we cannot settle for anything less than having open eyes, and it's why our hearts are thrilled when we gaze upon Beauty—whether in a book, a film, a dance, a song, a hike, a conversation, a kiss—because through all of those, we are touched by the echoes of eternity. We hear the Hidden Music.

I'm asking you to see things afresh—the way things were always intended to be seen. As Big. As Wonderful. As teeming with Life. To gain a vision for the Beauty of *your* every day. That crops can be used to feed our bodies, that music can sing and redeem almost every moment, that a cup of coffee can be a balm against a chaotic morning, that prayers ascend to the heavens and tug at the ear of God, that the Bible is God's voice to you—that's all Every Day Beauty. I'm asking you to view your life as *mythological*. Not as make-believe, not as pretend, but as the proper conception of the world.

> Even when real clouds or trees had been the material of the vision, they had been so only by reminding me of another world; and I did not like the return to ours. But now I saw the bright shadow coming out of the book into the real world and resting there, transforming all common things and yet itself unchanged. Or, more accurately, I saw the common things drawn into the bright shadow.[2]

Jesus is the Bright Shadow, that which looms over everything, transforming all common things—well, less transforming them, and more revealing to us just how *uncommonly* Beautiful His World is. This is the method of Beauty, of True Beauty. It reminds us of another world, a Better World, a Lasting City, and orients our whole self toward it. I say *it*, but I mean *Him*. And as Beauty beckons us, calls to us, everything it touches is transformed. Beauty is the framework by which we are welcomed into the True Reality.

Have eyes to see
the Beauty of Jesus in all His Creation.

Chapter 32

All Three, Together

OUR ROAD TRIP continued south, down to Kilkenny, and then farther to Cork. Each day was filled with driving, and we split the travel into sections with hikes and meals. It's the late afternoon, and as we're making our way to Cork we see some ruins of an abbey on the side of the road. We park, pulled off on a patch of gravel, and hop the stone fence. Surrounding the abbey is a bright-green field and there are cows and sheep grazing. The abbey stands tall against the field, and the clouds are outlined by the burning reds of a sleepy sun. Closer and closer, you can see the moss and vines crawling their way through the broken stone.

The abbey's roof is gone, but the stone walls and columns, the enormous arched windows, remain, all lined with lichen and greenery. Stone archways, some thirty feet high, welcome us from room to room. And its layout, the entire abbey, is in the shape of a cross. We're walking, exploring, taking in the stonework, and from the windows, we're taking in the rolling emerald countryside. The last scattered beams of day are shining through the window in the main room, shadows cast all around us by high walls. We stand there, together, basking in it. And imagining what this place meant.

The Beauty of it came first, and I did some reading about it later, seeing that the theological principles behind its construction were based on a kind of *architecture of light,* an invitation to raise the vision from the beauty of the material to the beauty of the immaterial. But it's not just the beauty of this abbey; I'm thinking of the Truth of it—the layout of the cross, the theology that not only comingled with the architecture, but the prayers and readings that echoed through this place. And then I'm wondering about how this Beauty, how this Truth, influenced their living, not just their virtue toward each other in the abbey, but how it spread to the local community around them. We're standing in the same place as many monks and nuns, some hundreds of years previous, and maybe we're all thinking the same things, how Beauty and Truth and Goodness shape everything.

And that's *how* we need to picture Beauty, Truth, and Goodness—the Transcendentals—as interdependent and, to use a ten-dollar word, a kind of *perichoresis,* an interpenetrating. These are not *separate* ideas; they depend upon each other. Beauty depends on Truth and Goodness, or put another way, everything that is truly beautiful will be good and true.

This is the Transcendental reality we live in, one we can't help but live in. Deny it all we want, but the draw is still felt upon our bodies; we long for more Truth, for more Goodness, for more Beauty. We long for Truth, for discovery of self, of other, of reality. We long for Goodness, for wholeness, for peace on earth and good will toward men. We long for Beauty, for our whole self to be consumed by it, swept up on a chariot of fire *into* it. And we feel it, know it deep within ourselves, when we deviate from this Transcendental Reality.

This is the foundation for becoming a Saint. It's living in unison with Jesus, in accord with the Cosmos as He created it, Good and Beautiful and True. It's about the pursuit of Life by denying everything in us that deviates from God's created order. And that's what makes every moment matter—every decision is infinite; every situation contains multitudes. It's why every time I chose alcohol as a savior, it destroyed me. It's why the isolation crippled me. It's why the anger and apathy ravaged my soul. And it's why the Good choices, the True ones, the Beautiful ones, began to heal me. The same responsibility lies upon your shoulders; there are no mediocre moments, no small decisions; everything is about Life and Death.

Embodied Transcendence
is the essence of Sainthood.

Chapter 33

Like Body, Like Soul

AFTER OUR TIME in Cork, we went to Kenmare, and then we drove up round the coast to Galway and stopped off at the Cliffs of Moher. You drive down narrow roads, rolling meadows on both sides, the stone fences, sheep in the fields; it's idyllic, postcard kind of stuff. Our white car is bouncing along the road, and we park and pack up, and begin on the trail. You see these places in photos, you even hear people talk about them when they're back from vacations, but you never really know what it's like to *be* there until it's your boots in the mud, until it's the salt spray on your face, until you catch yourself, mouth open, standing still, just staring. Those are the times you wish you could fly, could run to the jagged, grassy edge and just leap. Soar for a moment along the craggy cliffside, drop down to the foaming swirl splashing up against brown rock. You could breathe it all in, the magic, and we're holding hands as we walk the thin trail that follows the curve of the precipice.

Aislinn says, "Why not Spain?"

Out of the blue, and I ask what she means.

"Our visa runs out in February," she says. "We don't need to go back to Canada after. We could just spend a few months in Spain. I'll still teach; you can still do design."

"It's cheaper than Toronto," I say. And that seemed to make sense to both of us.

And I recognize that this was a rare time, almost a time outside of time. That it is not the norm—not yours and honestly, not mine either—this wasn't a common occurrence. But it became part of my journey. And our journeys will not be the same; what matters is what we learn from them.

So, after our return from Ireland to England, and after another wonderful three months there, with more stories than I can recount, and after some tear-filled goodbyes, that's what we did.

We went to Spain.

After landing in Valencia, with our backpacks and small suitcases, we take a bus a few hours along the southeast coast. We're riding along the Balearic Sea, and that feeds into the Mediterranean. Aislinn and I are split up on the bus since tickets are randomly assigned; she's resting, and I'm a few rows back doing some writing. Our time in England was a complete reshaping, but not the kind you can put a pin in, or label, or prescribe. Rebuilding, at least the attempt of it, is a lot less like pouring foundations for a house and following some blueprints. It's more like starting a garden; it's more about preparing the land, cultivating it, getting the right ingredients—the sun, the water, the fertile soil—and then . . . you wait.

Patiently.

Every day it's the same thing: the same tending, the long-suffering care, the weeding, the tilling, the watering. I couldn't place it, but within me there was a new calm. A peace. Not the frantic numbing of my self-medication, not the frenetic investigation for answers and rubrics and dogmas, not a frenzied hunt for a new set of rules, external manifestations of maturity. Just a peace. I'd do the work and let it be. That's what happened in England. Somewhere, in between pints with friends, chalk-dusted hands and scraped shins from the gym; somewhere while on walks down cobbled laneways, smoking in botanical gardens, having dinners around the fires in the living rooms of people we will never forget; somewhere in the midst of all of that, I forgot. I forgot the rush, the clamor, the desperation. And I settled into a peace I didn't quite understand. A symphony of embodiment, to the tune of the Hidden Music.

The path into this starts the same for all of us, the deciding to be found by Jesus, to follow the Hidden Music, to become a Saint. My story, my journey, is not yours, and I do not know where yours will take you, but I know where it leads. I also do not know what God will use to help all the scales fall from your eyes, but I want you to know it doesn't need to be some grand and exotic thing. Remember, every moment is infinite, and saying yes to God while you place your baby into her crib is just as potent as saying yes and quitting the dysfunctional job. Saying yes is watching the ordinary, embodied glory of your senior starting in his final lacrosse game, and it's just as powerful as saying yes and seeing the Transcendent Beauty of Truth in the ruins of an Irish abbey. Every moment is an opportunity, and every moment is transformed in the Bright Shadow of Jesus.

We're riding the winding roads and as we all sway with the sharp turns, everything in me keeps settling into its proper place. But we've got miles to go before we sleep.

We get to Calpe around nine at night, and the owners of our rental flat call us and say they will pick us up from the station; that it's a long walk. They're originally from Poland and their Spanish is a bit tough for me to understand, partly because I'm rusty and partly because of the accent. Everything comes at a bit of a delay, that few-seconds hesitation when you have to think over your words because you have to translate them in your head. The city lights are reflecting off our windows, and in the rhythmic lighting, spaced out by streetlamps, we can see each other's faces.

It's the end of February and it's dark as we unpack and head up the elevator with our hosts. The halls are dark, and our place on the eighth floor is lit by a small pot-light. They unlock the door and lead us in. It's a smallish one-bedroom condo, and both the bedroom and the living room have walk-out balconies. They leave us the keys, and there's a bottle of wine, a welcome card, and some Polish treats on the dining room table. All we do is strip down and hop into bed for a sleep.

I'm awake before Aislinn, heading out to the living room to start a pot of coffee. The zigzagged-circle filter in, the grinds on top, some water in the reservoir, and then that humming gurgle of water feeding through the drip heating tube. The sun is singing its way through the drawn blinds, and I pull them back to check out the balcony. And I see it.

Rolling waves highlighted by morning beams. White shores. Palm trees line the roads. A promenade along the beach shore, shops and restaurants the whole way down. And to our right, looking south from our balcony, we could see Ifach, a blocky mountain in the national park, maybe about a five-minute walk away. When Aislinn gets up, she joins me on the balcony, and we're sipping our coffees, and we're in awe of it all.

Bodies teach souls;
tune them to the Hidden Music of Jesus.

Chapter 34

You Are What You Love

FOUR DAYS A week we hike that mountain—after a morning coffee and a game of cards, and back in time for Ais to teach in the afternoon. Up the gravel road to the entrance; through the garden and past the hut with information about the park; through a small cave, a tunnel, wet with runoff and mossy. And then it's just the winding, stony, steep path to the top. Every time we'd do this it became more familiar, and more enjoyable. You learned the path, the solid rocks, the branches to grab onto as you pulled up the trail. I'd teach Aislinn Spanish, and we'd talk about our past year and what we were going to do next. At the summit we'd have breakfast, we'd pet the stray cats that climbed to the top, hunting seagulls. We'd help tourists take their pictures. It was an easy rhythm to slip into, a structure that gave us hours to talk, to think, to practice. And the inclines got easier, our legs got stronger, our footing more secure.

That hike framed our day, differently than other rhythms we'd done previously. It was physical, it was communal, it was vulnerable, it was engaging us where we were at in every way. We were beholding an ever-unfolding beauty—the bright sea, the white stone, the rusted earth. Meals and rest at the top. It was an overlap of just about everything that mattered to us. Not an overlap, a weaving together, an amplification. Joys multiplied, sort of thing.

This was a liturgy, a sacred ritual, an external form. It was something we did that also did something to us. A kind of catechism of the body. And when I saw so clearly that these hikes were a kind of living liturgy, I began to see how everything else I did was the same. It wasn't just Spain. It's not only England. It's everything. It's all the same, using our bodies as a way to teach our entire person. What we do, and we do what we love, shapes our values and reveals our priorities. It casts light on what we believe to be Good and True and Beautiful. Everything is a self-portrait—a reflection of who we truly are. "You are what you love."[1]

Everything is a liturgy, a way you use your body to teach your whole self what matters most. What you do when you wake up or are on your way to work, the shows and movies and social media you consume, it all shapes you. When you run to your phone first thing in the morning, you're teaching yourself what matters most. I did the same thing with a tumbler of bourbon—I was using my body, creating a habit, that then taught my whole self *what* could help me in my times of pain. But so, too, are there positive liturgies, space we can carve out, ways to use our bodies to teach us to *become* Saints. Our every embodied action teaches us and reveals us. Makes the invisible visible.

Years previous, when I was in seminary, I had taken a course on Old Testament biblical theology—*biblical*, here, referring to the theology of particular books with respect to their place in the whole metanarrative, the Big Story. The idea was to seek to understand what's being communicated in light of chronology and historical setting and the unfolding development of God's plan of redemption. We were in class, and on my desk was just a pen and a spiral-bound notebook. My professor had an overhead projector on, and you could see dust along the beams of light shining on the screen. He had a list of five viewpoints, which shone through one of those transparency sheets. Each of them was a different take on what Genesis meant when it talks about being made in the Image of God.

He was going through each one, marking up the sheet with blue pen and red pen, casting shadows on every wall. He was telling us what was wrong with all the systematic views of image and likeness and then started to tell us a bit about the Ancient Near Eastern context; about how people used those terms, *image* and *likeness*, around the same time Genesis was written. He told us that in ancient Egypt kings were *living* statues of a god; they were some kind of behavioral reflection of the god. It wasn't focused on appearance, he said—a male king could be in the image of a female god—it was about character, and about embodying that character to the people. This being in the image, he told us, has to do with *sonship*, a family bond. About reflecting God's character because of relationship. That essentially sums up everything to do with image. Sonship: right relationship and a proper reflection.[2]

Genesis carries this idea, but it's not reserved for kings alone. All of humanity, so says the Good Book, is made in the Image of God. All of us are made for Divine Relationship, to Love God and enjoy His Love. And each of us is a kind of Divine Icon, a physical representation of who He is, sharing in His Rule of the cosmos. That's the invitation: that we would join Him in bringing order—His order, His Goodness, Truth, and Beauty—to the world around us. We do that *from* Love, *from* relationship; and we do it *by* seeking to be like Him. We are His representatives to our neighbors, our coworkers, our spouses, our kids, everyone. We show God to the world around us through our bodies, by living and loving as He would.

The vision is one of cosmic unity; God intends to rule *with* and *through* humanity, not primarily from the perspective of King and servant but as Father with children. It is a relational context of Love. In order for us, each of us, to be Good imagers, we need to know God, to understand Him and relate to Him. We need to live in His Life so as to express it. This is the core of who we are as humans; that's the ontological idea communicated. Who we are, our primary identity, is an imager—designed for divine Love and for expressing that divine Love.

And that was a belief, a frame of being, that stirred me, in my mind but also in my guts; it set my heart ablaze. It conformed me, not to *my* reality but to God's Reality. It gave me the path, the framework for living. To be an imager. Same thing as being a Saint. Interchangeable. To *be* the kind of person who loves God, enjoys that Love, and does whatever possible to express that Love.

That's what's on my mind during these morning hikes under a Spanish sun. The thoughts of all these liturgies, these ways of being, that shaped my beliefs. Essentially, I was trying to wed my old framework of *spiritual living* with being a real, physical manifestation of God on earth. This wasn't comparing apples and oranges, it was comparing phantoms and frames, ghosts and corpses. Ghosts can't fulfill the Sermon on the Mount, but neither can a cadaver. I needed a harmony, one that went beyond the functional Gnosticism that led me to mediocrity; I needed to know the *how* of this Saintly call.

Aislinn is teaching English again some afternoon, and I'm out for a walk along the beach, listening to a podcast. The salt water laps at my bare feet in small ebbing tides, the Spanish sun browns my shoulders and back, people smile and nod as we pass each other. I would walk this stretch, about a mile, back and forth, for a few hours while Aislinn taught. I'd listen to audiobooks and lectures, I'd listen to the sea and pray, I'd put on Coltrane and contemplate. I can't remember the podcast, but someone in it mentions John Paul II's *Theology of the Body*, saying that the cultural climate we live in now is so dire because we don't understand our bodies. And I'm thinking that I didn't understand my body. I lived in the no-man's-land between what I grew up in and around, and whatever *this* idea was. So I buy the Kindle version of the book, *Man and Woman He Created Them: A Theology of the Body* by Pope John Paul II.

I'm sitting on the curved brick wall, beach and shore and sea below my dangling legs, cobblestone promenade at my back. Spaniards are tanning and playing volleyball all around me; they're drinking beers out of coolers and they're laughing. Behind me tourists are buying paella and postcards and sweaters with Calpe on it. And I'm reading this:

> The structure of this body is such that it permits him to be the author of genuine human activity. . . . The body expresses the

person. It is thus, in all its materiality ("he formed man with dust of the ground"), penetrable and transparent, as it were, in such a way as to make it clear who man is and who he ought to be.[3]

And then, I'm reading on:

> There is a strong link between the mystery of creation, as a gift that springs from Love, and that beatifying "beginning" of man's existence as male and female, in the whole truth of their bodies. . . . When the first man exclaims at the sight of the woman, "she is flesh from my flesh and bone from my bones" (Gen 2:23), he simply affirms the human identity of both. By exclaiming this, he seems to say, *Look, a body that expresses the "person!"* . . . This "body" reveals the "living soul." . . . This is the body: a witness to creation as a fundamental gift, and therefore a witness to Love as the source from which this giving springs.[4]

It's hard to describe what happened to me that day, reading that tome on my phone, having just about everything else settle into place. We live and move and interact with the whole world *through* our bodies; we are not souls that drive corpse cars around. The body is at unity with the soul. "Man is not a man without his body, just as he is not a man without his soul. A corpse is not a man, but also a ghost is not a man."[5] Bodies aren't simply biological, flesh and blood; bodies are theological, revelations of the soul and the expression of the Love from which we find our source. This flew in the face of the materialism, the spiritualism, the dualism that I saw in the world around me, and that I saw far too often in the church (with just a sprinkling of Jesus on top). This was not a faulty understanding of humans, it wasn't a bad anthropology. It was a theological one—a creedal one, a New Lore. Well, new to me, but as old as Creation itself.

These bodies, the ones we tend to hate or malign, the ones we treat poorly and feel ashamed of, were so much more. All those faulty views led to polarized, extreme versions of indulgence and asceticism; they corrupted that body-soul *unity*, placing the soul higher up on the value chart. So much higher, in fact, that the normal urges and cravings and passions of the body were seen as deficient; so we killed them, or at least lied about killing them. All in the pursuit of Sainthood. But I hope you can see now, as I did then, that this body I have, the body you have, is an expression of Divine Love. The passions and cravings I have—for sex and food, for thrill and sleep, for competition and camaraderie, for hugs and mastery—are all part of the package. These reveal that I long for the Good, the True, and the Beautiful; and as I use my body in the way it was created to be used, I find more and more Joy, because I'm brought closer and closer to the Source. My body reveals my soul, and it reveals that I'm a person who desires to *be* a Saint, a man who lives in the Divine Love and expresses it.

I'm looking around, and there's couples hugging, and I'm thinking about how *that* reveals the Divine Love. I see people swimming, and I'm thinking the same. I'm starting to wonder just *how* it is that I've missed this; how did I see the body as prison, rather than Gift?

Bodies are theological, intended to be an Icon of God.

Chapter 35

An Archetype for Being

A FEW DAYS later, Aislinn is teaching, I'm done with my design projects, and there's an old hermitage to check out on the other side of Old Town. The city, Calpe, is mostly white stone, and in Old Town, the ground is either tiled mosaic or small stones cemented together. The houses have cast-iron balcony railings and I'm walking the narrow laneways as people hang their laundry out over the alley. My back is sweating because the walls hold the heat of the sun, like furnaces. The old city is quiet, some men are smoking on a patio, and I'm on my way to the Hermitage of San Salvador. Truth be told, I wish I could tell you it was stunning, to fit the picturesque vibe of the rest of the city, but it wasn't what I expected.

The sun had scorched a lot of the greenery and so what should have been a welcoming garden just seemed unkempt and forgotten. To get to the top of the hill, you had to walk a winding stone pathway, round the mountain, slowly inclining, until the summit. That's where the small white building was; that's where you could go to pray. And that was my path. As I'm going up, along the inclined staircase, white stones in patterns in the cement, I notice a stone frame on a stone post, standing about five feet high. I lean and peek inside and I see a kind of icon of Jesus standing before Pilate, being condemned to death. The stations of the cross, staggered at intervals along this winding path as preparation for a time of prayer on the summit.

You see these depictions of Jesus, God become man, and frame by frame, you see Jesus, in and through His body, expressing Divine Love. The next frame shows Jesus carrying His cross. Farther up, dried brush draping over the ascending stairs, you see Jesus falling, you see His face being wiped, you see Him stripped, you see the nails, you see Him die, you see Him laid in a tomb.

Each step I'm taking reveals His story, and it hits me. Jesus had a body. And through His body, with His body, Jesus expresses Divine Love. God embodied, the Word become flesh. My body is sweating in the dry heat, my mouth is caked and dry from the walk over and the walk up, and I'm thinking, meditating, on how, in the midst of His passion, Jesus thirsted. These things hit in waves, that Jesus had hands and fingers and a tongue, that His feet must have ached after long days walking, His back ached after carrying the cross—this was our similarity, our way of relation.

> The soul has nothing in common with God; there is no kinship between it and the divine. Its kinship is with its body, in virtue of their common creation, rather than with God.[1]

My kinship with Jesus is this embodied Reality we share; and it is in His incarnation that He makes known to us not just the Divine Love, and not just the deepest kind of relation, but a New Model for my *being*. He reveals the way to *be* embodied, the way to be truly human. When God "joined himself to us a new way of being human appeared."[2]

I'm taking the final steps, reaching the summit, and I see the hermitage, and there's an olive tree planted beside, a ring of stones at its base. And I'm thinking of the Mount of Olives, where Jesus embraced the cup, and I'm thinking about how Jesus drank the cup I deserved, and I drink the cup He deserved; and I'm thinking of Saint Athanasius:

> You know how it is when some great king enters a large city and dwells in one of its houses; because of his dwelling in that single house, the

whole city is honored, and enemies and robbers cease to molest it. Even so is it with the King of all; He has come into our country and dwelt in one body amidst the many, and in consequence the designs of the enemy against mankind have been foiled and the corruption of death, which formerly held them in its power, has simply ceased to be. For the human race would have perished utterly had not the Lord and Savior of all, the Son of God, come among us to put an end to death.[3]

The whole of us has been honored, the fullness of humanity emerges in the so-called Second Adam. Jesus is the architect of a New and True way of being human. The narratives we've read so many times, of Jesus and His living, are rich with this framework; the Kingdom of God drawing near and the physical embodiment of that Reality. And that's our invitation: to *be* the Body of Jesus; to be His hands and feet; to do as we see our Father doing. That in some small way, by seeing us, people will see Him. Jesus is Image fulfilled—perfect relationship with God and perfect expression of that Divine Love.

This embodiment is the mechanism by which we experience full communion with God.

ONE FOOT IN THE LIFE TO COME

I'm in the hermitage; it's terra-cotta tiled floors, white walls, wooden chairs, and on the back wall is a redbrick outcropping with a statue of the resurrected Jesus on it, staff in hand. There's a place to kneel and pray, and I do so. It smells ancient and like earth, and it's cool there, at the foot of Jesus, on the rust-colored tiles. My body relaxes a bit, shoulders drop, and I rub away a few beads of sweat on my brow. The reprieve from the Spanish sun. My soul feels that same rest, that same unfolding, the same submission, into the cool rest of Jesus' victory. A harmony of my whole being. I feel the unity, made to lie down in green pastures, so to speak. It's quiet, and I'm kneeling there, in that silence, waiting for some sacred moment. *That's what happens, right?* I'm thinking to myself. *You take the walk, the way of the cross, you think all these thoughts about Jesus and His passion and resurrection, and then you come in here, and you hear the voice of God.*

That's what I'm expecting.

And that's what I'm waiting for.

Trumpets or the sound of many rushing waters, bright lights and thundering. But all I have is this cool silence. So I linger longer; I wasn't an amateur, I know that good things happen to those who wait. I wanted a fact, something packageable and shareable, something to bookend everything I had felt. The infinite in a tidbit; the boundless as a slogan. Still, there's nothing. Just the smell of clay and dust, just the shade, just this quiet moment. I knew I couldn't wait forever, I wanted to be back for dinner with Aislinn, so I get up and I make the sign of the cross and I leave the hermitage, into the warm sun.

My eyes narrow and feel that tickling pang of adjusting; I feel a warmth on my skin, heating away its tightness, and I see the olive tree, leaves dancing on the wind. My body feels refreshed, a few moments in the cool, resting in a place of peace. Our bodies shape our perceptions; my tired and hot body found rest in the cool hermitage, and my weary soul found rest at the foot of Jesus. As I write that, I know it sounds like a slogan, like a tidbit, but that's not how it came about. I can't describe how I "learned" it because it was a feeling. Like cracking a beer after a day cutting the grass in the hot sun, it was something that needed to be lived, something encountered, something met with. I *met* with peace that day, body and soul. The reality was that my body prepared my soul for the peace. There's a reason, I assume, the way of the cross was winding, ascending, up a dry and sunny mount: It was an embodied liturgy. That was the revelation—the cooperation of body and soul by means of embodiment.

> Nothing can cure the soul but the senses, just as nothing can cure the senses but the soul.[4]

This same body, the one that carried me back down the mountain and through the city to my flat, was the one that was intended to *mirror* the Life to come. My body, the one that was growing hungry, the one that wanted water, the one that would need to sleep, was the reflection of the New Creation. How I used this body, how I lived and loved, would directly shape my perception of Life and New Creation, and the perception of those around me. I needed to learn to *become* the Light on a Hill, like that hermitage. I needed to learn what it meant to design an architecture for my body so as to shape and refine my soul.

There's a thought experiment you can do to help you understand this. Picture yourself: It's a cold, snowy day—the kind of wet, heavy snow that soaks you down to the bone. You're underdressed, and you're running late. You're freezing. Your hands are red and stiff from the cold. You're rushing to the bus or to an appointment, and you're cussing under your breath because you just got in an argument with your dad. As you run, you hit your hand on an iron fence. It stings, bad. You feel the throbbing pain, the ache, and you can't really shake it off.

Now picture a warm, sunny day. You're with your friends at a barbecue in the park, and a bunch of you are playing a game of football. You're laughing and playing and joking. You jump to catch a long throw, stub your finger on the ball, but still reach for the catch. You barely feel it as you land, ball in hand, running for the end zone.

How you are in your body shapes how you feel, even down to things like pain. Our bodies form our understanding of life; that's how they were made: to be the vehicle by which we truly interact with the world. What is needed, in order to be a Saint, is a Holy Imagination, a sanctified vision. One that sees clearly, one that pays attention to the constant homily of God's Creation.

Often, we're nearsighted, shaped primarily by the superficial vision of our circumstances and situations. That's too finite, too terrestrial; it's being blind to the infinite and the cosmic. Our vision is shaped by stubbed toes, by blown gaskets, by house bills, by relationship status, by phone calls with bad news. Those things blur our vision; they cause us to look at life and living in some myopic manner, reducing everything that happens to *only* that which can be seen. Materialism. Becoming a Saint is about seeing behind it all, seeing the Reality that makes up our world, and then partnering and participating in that Divine Reality.

All is opportunity.

It's a big responsibility, being human. We are images of the Divine, intended to express His Love. We use our bodies to do so, but we can't get lost in the mundane and the situational; we can't think that we need a Spanish hermitage near the Mediterranean so that we can embody the living realities of the Transcendental. All we need is our context, our situation, our community. Everyone around us, every moment of our lives, is the Kingdom plan of Jesus—places where we, and only we, have the opportunity to make manifest His Reality.

This is the revolution.

It's each of us embracing our identity, our calling, and our place. It's the revolt of Grace and Love. I imagine a world saturated and perforated by Saints, by those who turn to virtue rather than the bottom of a bottle, by those who look for salvation in the Truth, the Person of Jesus, rather than facts and definitions, by those who search for and are drowned in Beauty, rather than numbing the pain with every kind of distraction. I imagine a world where each moment is shaped by Gift—the chance to be transformed by Life through the embodiment of that Life. Grocery stores filled with patience, houses marked by peace, churches brimming with hospitality. None of it seeking to make a name for ourselves, nothing about building our platform, about pleasing a paying constituency; all of it about Kingdom, about transformation by beholding. From one degree of glory to another.

*God speaks, most often,
in His still, small voice; have ears to hear.*

A LITURGY OF EMBODIMENT

The soul's desire can only be satisfied by the Infinite Jesus.

Virtue, Goodness, is the practice of participating in God's Love.

Jesus is the lens for interpreting the Cosmos; understanding comes by intimacy.

Have eyes to see the Beauty of Jesus in all His Creation.

Embodied Transcendence is the essence of Sainthood.

Bodies teach souls; tune them to the Hidden Music of Jesus.

Bodies are theological, intended to be an Icon of God.

God speaks, most often, in His still, small voice; have ears to hear.

Act V.
The Melody of New Beginnings

Chapter 36

The Heavenly Cadence

WHEN MY JOURNEY began, I didn't know that I was living out all kinds of liturgies of Death, wondering why I kept getting so close to the precipice. Wondering why I just wanted *out*. My rhythms—the drinking, the numbing, the working myself ragged—formed me. They taught my body what to orient itself around. My life was liturgical, ceremonial, and it shaped my soul. All of life is liturgical, every last bit; and the habits, routines, tendencies, and practices we commit to, mindlessly or not, form us. We talk often of spiritual formation, but we forget that it's happening *all* the time. Every time I reached for the bottle when I felt pain, loneliness, or sorrow I was teaching myself, etching it into the fiber of my *being*, that this was salvation.

That's what liturgies do—they carve new impulses into our skin and heart and soul; they create and develop desires and motives. It's secret work, behind the scenes, a drop at a time. But it all, eventually, changes you. Soon, you don't even think about grabbing whatever your proverbial bottle of booze is; you've already taught yourself, ingrained it into your whole ethos, that when the pain comes, this is what you do. Not everyone is an alcoholic, not everyone gives into apathy, and not everyone lets the anger burn; but we all have our coping mechanisms, our ways of self-medicating, and those things shape us. And what we do with our bodies shapes what we do with our beliefs. It's the house of our own making. Existential.

That's what hit me, hard. I *looked* like I was altogether the poster boy of a good little Christian, but the rhythm of my life, my habits, betrayed something altogether different. It's easy to think, *I'm okay because everyone thinks I'm okay.* But all that really means is that I'm good at hiding. And that all I care about is false perceptions, not reality. Oh, the little lies I told myself.

The full circle was realizing that the same free will I used to dig my own grave would be needed to cultivate a living garden. The full circle was the epiphany that I needed to do what Jesus said: clean the inside and let the outside deal with itself.[1] The full circle was that the Truth mattered, not the lies I told to help myself sleep better at night, not the deceit I used to find some semblance of love and acceptance. The full circle was learning that my *body* told me this—before I fell asleep I knew I wasn't okay. I felt the fear of being seen, I felt the exhaustion in my bones, like all my strength was sapped. I knew the anxiety of keeping up appearances, the concern of needing to play the part, and the dread of being found out. The full circle was the invitation out of that way of life and into the Good, Honest Truth. No matter what it cost. The full circle was realizing that I need to work backward, not forward.

What I am trying to say is what I wrote in my journal while living in Spain:

Feel your humanity. The tension of bones that snap, of shoulders that bend, of hearts that break. Feel your fragility before a wind that sweeps away. Time pumps through your veins, and each day we face shadows, we face devils, we face Death. I will one day lose. I shall be bested, my body will fail. My heart. My lungs. My whole self. Gone. Dust in the storm. Feel that, your humanity. Feel the finite and the frail, the shelf life of the body. And feel the strength it takes to Live. Feel the courage required to Die, to be Buried, to be Forgotten. Because when a seed is planted in the ground and dies, a harvest comes. I climb out of the grave, emerge as a flower, on an old corpse. Blooming. Not invincible, not perfect, not impervious. I blossom in a weakness that reveals a strength.

That was me learning the liturgy of my body. My body gave me a framework, it gave me sensations and impressions into what it needed, what I needed. My body tells me I am finite. My body tells me, in overlapping intervals, that I need sleep, food, air. My body tells me when I'm tired, hungry, thirsty, sick, scared, lonely, and hurt. My body tells me when I'm happy, when I'm comfortable; I smile and laugh, I cry and wince. Part of embodying Goodness, Truth, and Beauty is recognizing that we do so with our bodies, and that, while each of us *is* a body, our bodies and our needs are different. That comparison, trying to measure up to another person's living, is often opposed to *hearing*. It is trying to abide by their liturgy of the body, not hearing your own body's needs.

A short walk from our flat in Spain was the beach we went to most often. The supermarket was a short walk again on the way home. That beach had a place for calisthenics—monkey bars, pull-up bars, parallel bars for dips and gymnastic stuff—and we would jog there a few times a week. I'd put on a podcast and do a workout under the palms, golden sun shining, saltwater air. It'd be small circuits of pull-ups and push-ups and squat jumps and dips and core. Over and over and over. All working out is, in some sense, the same: the continual confrontation with weakness, and pushing through it. To move the threshold. To get weak after ten, fifteen, twenty, thirty pull-ups by doing them over and over, when your forearms throb, your hands ache, and your back is on fire. The total number goes up, bit by bit, week by week, month by month. And you get stronger.

People would come and go, doing their own workouts. All of us doing our best with a few sets of iron bars. Some guys would come and rip off a few sets of who knows how many pull-ups, and some guys would come and do one. But each of us was facing our weakness, using our bodies to become stronger. Comparison was the enemy of growth; I couldn't compare myself to the Adonis whose strength made it look like his two-hundred-pound body was weightless. All I had was my body and the places I needed to get strong, directly relating to all the places where I was weak. I had a bum knee, an injury borne out of the culmination of hockey, soccer, and running. I had to do physical therapy for it, had to temper my squats. This I know, for my body told me so.

When it comes to developing liturgies for our bodies, ways to get us up out of the pit, to center around Life, and not Death, we tend to get blanket statements, the broad brush, the generalizations. We tend to get a narrow path, abstract yet absolute. And then we compare when we don't do it like the Strongmen of the Faith. We think that we're not doing enough because we don't pray a certain amount of hours a day, because we don't read a certain amount of Bible chapters in a week, because we don't fast enough, take time for solitude enough. And that's easy, because spiritual formation is often packaged and sold exploiting our insecurities, our not-enoughness. And these so-called Strongmen know we look up to them, so they package their routine as a program and sell it to us. But that's all wrong.

You and I know what we need to do: Read your Bible, pray every day, and you'll grow, grow, grow. But we don't listen, and we don't follow. We don't listen to our bodies, that maybe we are a bit weaker than we imagined. That we need a shorter prayer, *Lord Jesus Christ, Son of God, have mercy on me, a sinner.* That we need to start with a psalm, or a proverb, or a short gospel chapter. That we need to build up the strength, that we need to develop a liturgy of Life, and that part of that is the constant *killing* of the Liturgies of Death.

I should also say that the *narrow path* here is not an allusion to Matthew 7:14, but a kind of constricted view of what makes up formation. Yes, Truth shapes us. Truth is part of what forms a full and robust liturgy. But we need more. We need Good liturgies, Beautiful liturgies; ways of being that speak to our whole self. How many of us have read a book, heard a sermon, listened to a podcast that laid a foundation for teaching our bodies with Beauty? With Goodness and virtue? Very few, is my guess. We settle for that which is prescriptible. But to be molded and shaped by the wild adventure of Beauty? To be reconstituted by the rigors of Goodness? That is a different game entirely. You see, rhythms, liturgies, are invitations, not competitions. They are ways we summon our body, our self, into the Life to come.

Formation is not competition, it is offering loaves and fish and having God multiply.

Chapter 37

Crafting a Holy Imagination

MY BODY IS hiking up, up over roots and stones, the early beams of morning warming the same skin that's being cooled from the sea breeze; my mind is back in seminary in a pneumatology class, a class on the theology of the Holy Spirit. We're beginning to tackle the topic of the Trinity, of Saint Basil of Caesarea and his book *On the Holy Spirit*, and I was overcome, as by the Muses, with a question. I lean to my friend beside me, and I'm asking *how* these old Saints, the fathers of the church, came up with these ideas. *How* did they piece them together, the puzzle of what was revealed, into a True and cohesive whole? He started answering, but his answer assumed the some 1,700 years of church history that had passed since Saint Basil's work. What I wanted to know, what I wanted to participate in, was the kind of thinking, the kind of being alive, that led further into Truth.

How did these church fathers think?

So I put my hand up, pen in my fingers, and my professor says, "Yes, Josh?" and I ask about this *way* of thinking.

And he pauses for a second, and then he says, "What you're asking about is imagination, a Holy Imagination. It's an originality and an artistry, and it's sanctified." And he moved on, going back to the scriptural proofs for the Holy Spirit being God. And I wrote that down, a sanctified imagination, artistry made holy. Class came to a close and he called me up to the front.

"You'd be interested in C. S. Lewis on this," he says. "His thoughts on imagination will probably help you get where you want to go."

And that was it.

And off I went to scour all the unread Lewis essays I could get my hands on.

On the other side of the city, I'm remembering as we hike farther up, there was an old books library and a Cambridge printing of some of Lewis's select literary essays. That was stop number one. And maybe it was sheer good fortune, or something else, but when I found the book, sat at the desk, and opened it, "Bluspels and Flalansferes: A Semantic Nightmare" caught my eye. I started reading:

> It will have escaped no one that in such a scale of writers the poets will take the highest place; and among the poets those who have at once the tenderest care for old words and the surest instinct for the creation of new metaphors.[1]

And I began to wonder why the poets took the highest place in Lewis's mind, concerning the creation of new metaphors. Why was it the arts that began to answer the deepest questions?

> But it must not be supposed that I am in any sense putting forward the imagination as the organ of truth. We are not talking of truth, but of meaning: meaning which is the antecedent condition both of truth and falsehood, whose antithesis is not error but nonsense.[2]

Maybe the poets were playing a different game. They desired meaning first, and they assumed that Truth was bound up in that meaning. My questions continued. I can still remember the smell of the desk I sat at, it was old and oak, in a row, with halogen overhead lamps. The library was dimly lit, scattered beams of color shining through a stained glass window, the lignin of the old books in the air. That's the binder in the wood-based paper, the mix of must and vanilla. And I'm asking about meaning and metaphor, about what forms belief. And Lewis was answering, talking to me, like it was a conversation:

> I am a rationalist. For me, reason is the natural organ of truth; but imagination is the organ of meaning. Imagination, producing new metaphors or revivifying old, is not the cause of truth, but its condition. . . . And thence, I confess, it does follow that if our thinking is ever true, then the metaphors by which we think must have been good metaphors.[3]

I didn't need to parse through everything Lewis meant by *rationalist*, *reason*, or even *condition*; what I wanted to work through was his idea of meaning. And that, in his mind, if we have some human semblance of truth, some way of living the Good Life, of being virtuous, it must mean that our *metaphors* were also Good; that our symbols and analogies, our mythos, was of the right kind. The two go hand in hand, a virtuous Life and the metaphors of meaning. And since he's a rationalist, it wasn't chance that got us to that harmony of metaphysical metaphor and virtue.

And he continues to help me understand:

> It does follow that if those original equations, between good and light, or evil and dark, between breath and soul and all the others, were from the beginning arbitrary and fanciful . . . then all our thinking is nonsensical. But we cannot, without contradiction, believe it to be nonsensical. And so, admittedly, the view I have taken has metaphysical implications. But so has every view.[4]

And that implication is the Source, something that stands behind and before Reality, imbuing it with meaning. If the old stories, the old poems, the old myths and creeds, if they were nothing but arbitrary, then every mode of being, including thinking, follows suit. It's all chance. But that doesn't seem to be the case; it seems that our lives are rational, ordered, beautiful, and good, and therefore, the metaphysical view Lewis ascribes to is that the metaphors that shape our meaning are also True, Good, and Beautiful. The symbols are True.

And we're nearing the summit, and there's the same cats to pet, a new group of people wanting pictures, and there's the view. *A Holy Imagination*, I'm thinking, as I peel an orange, seated, looking out over the sea, *is one that breathes new Life into: into meaning, into living and loving, into our very worldview.* There's another whisper, another bit of guidance from these old Saints, who left their words in books as signposts to mark the way.

You have to be able to imagine lives that are not yours.[5]

Wendell Berry said that, and he means that we need to conceptualize a way of living that is beyond where we currently stand. It's why fairy tales matter so much, not just for the kids who find in them heroes to emulate but for adults who, if they have eyes to see, will envision the cosmos afresh. Envision a person, a Saint, we just might become. "Fairy tales are more than true: not because they tell us that dragons exist, but because they tell us that dragons can be beaten."[6]

We always rested at the top, had short conversations with people who had come to see the view, and lots of them were from out of country. We drank water, took a few moments to refresh, and in between visits with other hikers, Aislinn and I are together but thinking in our own worlds. She used this time the same as I did, as a time to contemplate.

I'm peeling another orange and a cat hops along the rocks, hunting for seagulls, its own midmorning snack. I'm thinking that Holy Imaginations, minds and hearts and souls and bodies saturated in the Beautiful story of God, are the tools of transformation. It's not naivety, and it's not the power of positive thinking; it's not pretending pain doesn't hurt by bluffing our way into some platitude. A Holy Imagination transforms by a more True interpretation of Reality, not a diminishing. Holy Imaginations imbue our whole lives, the good and bad, the better and the worse, with significance. With meaning. It's almost too hard to explain this because we live in a time that sells trite significance, meaning by slogan—and this is not that. This is the Real kind, not a sweatshop knockoff; it's the mythos of the Saint. The ability to behold, and therefore to become. The imagination to see a Life, a full Life, a kind of Life that bursts with love and joy and peace, no matter what comes—and then to *become* the person who lives that Life. To imagine the knight slaying the dragon, and then embody courage; to imagine the Saint, facing all manner of hell with a smile and clear eyes, and then to embody that loving loyalty. Our dragons are not often scaled and fire-breathing; but be sure we face dragons every day, and someone needs to slay them.

We're making the descent, down the winding slopes, the mountainside emanating the heat it's gathered from the morning sun. All you can hear are the cries of gulls, the faint ebbs of the sea below, and the crunching earth beneath our boots. I'm still thinking, my body engaged, and this repetitive rhythm invites my mind into a kind of contemplative space. We face every kind of malice on our Journey into Sainthood, and we need to imagine, behold, *how* a Saint acts, *what* a Saint does *before* we arrive. Because we arrive bit by bit, opportunity by opportunity.

That is my story, I'm thinking. And it will be yours too. We don't arrive all at once, there is no *real* moment of stark change. Change comes like food, nourishing, making us strong, day by day. "If you can change the way people think. . . . The way they see themselves. The way they see the world. If you do that, you can change the way people live their lives."[7] And that's how we do it; we relearn who we are, as Saints, and then our lives are changed. We imagine the most True, Good, and Beautiful kind of person and then we embody that person; formed and shaped by Wonder.

Holy Imaginations saturate life with opportunity for embodied Sainthood.

Chapter 38

Working Backward from Heaven

WE ARE EATING fish and rice and sautéed veggies and drinking some wine on our eighth-floor patio. Night is falling, slowly, and the gulls are soaring on the gentle breeze, purples painting the sky. We're talking and laughing. It was a kind of heaven on earth: Hidden Music. Lamplights slowly turn on, their dull amber glow casting circles on the promenade. After dinner we decide to go for a walk, down to the Cala el Raco, along a stony beach at the base of Ifach.

To get there, we walk through a tight part of town, narrow roads and white and yellow stone shops and houses. Everything glowing orange in the evening, lit by hanging lights and sconces. There is Spanish jazz in the air, playing out of so many cafés and restaurants. The stray cats walk the road beside us, and we're holding hands as we pass the last restaurant on our way to the lookout. The beach here isn't sand; it's giant, jagged rocks, stretching out some hundred feet into the sea. Foam swirls and froths between the rocks as waves clap against those farthest out. You can watch the water weave through the nooks and crannies, little rapids spilling out into pools. Aislinn and the stray cats are jumping along the rocks, and I'm smoking a cigar, seated on a rock closer to the walkway. The cobalt curtain of night falls and the stars come out. The far shore and the hilled city is lit by hundreds of beacons, houses and bars open. The sea flickers, reflecting the glow. And again I'm thinking, *Heaven on earth*.

And that's the goal, the point of it all. To bring heaven to earth, to live with the Life to come as the *telos*. That night, sitting in the mahogany smell of my cigar, the salty spindrift on my skin, watching the silhouette of my wife and the cats, it made sense. Heaven was the framework, and my life was to be lived by its cadence. There's no program for this, no lists, no particularities, no subscription plans, no twelve-week studies. Heaven meeting earth is the culmination of the whole story, the Kingdom made manifest, Myth become Substance.

How?

Work backward from heaven.

It doesn't need to be sunsets on a ragged Spanish beach. I only saw it then because it was so obvious, but because I saw it then, I could look back and see all the ways God had been inviting me, showing me ways to *work backward from heaven*—to live in His Reality. When God's Kingdom meets earth, it does so, first, as the Person of Jesus, and Kingdom is about reign and rule. That means most of our life needs to be a kind of body and soul reorientation to *that* Kingdom. A submission, but not as loss, as Divine Expansion. Heaven meets earth, not just in the beauty of a wife jumping on rocks in the spray of the sea but in all our decisions to embody Goodness, Truth, and Beauty. In the ways we open our homes and share our tables with those in need, in the ways we choose kindness and Grace and forgiveness in the middle of raging fights, in the way we stand firm for what is eternal, in a world tossed to and fro by every changing wind of belief. Attitudes matter, motivations matter, and everything, every bit of our lives, is this opportunity to bring heaven to earth, to spread Jesus' reign of Love.

Think of fullness, imagine substance, imagine Beauty up from ashes, dream of all things made new. And then imagine your whole life, all of your living, governed by that Reality. When I say *your*, I mean it. You, personally. What does *your* living need to become? What does *your* life change into? How is church transformed? Community?

Career? Relationships? Loneliness? Joy? What if, based on all this, based on these ideas of identity, of Truth and Goodness and Beauty, on Virtue, on Becoming, on Embodiment, on Imagination, you developed your own rhythm of life? What if you took ownership, were responsible for your gifts, your calling, your desires?

And what if, from this foundation, from this new Reality, from this Source, you let yourself dream as big as possible and then pursued it with everything you had? What if you were honest, confronted all the darkness within you, all the selfishness, all the ways you live out Liturgies of Death, and committed to renewal? Committed to a vivification process? What if you imagined all you could be, all that created and designed potential, all those talents within you, longing to be multiplied, to transform you and the world around you, and what if you leaned in?

What if you became?

What if you took the first step, of thousands, toward becoming a Saint?

And sure, there are the tried and tested and true methods: You can read your Bible, you can search our rich tradition and history for all kinds of details on prayer, fasting, Bible reading, solitude, contemplation, and everything else. This book is less the *how-to* of spiritual formation and more along the lines of *why-be* a Saint, with some wisdom gathered from the path. The rough and brutal, the downs and the outs, but also, what can happen, even to someone as broken and easily swayed as me. I am no Saint, not yet. I am no guru, no sage, no man to build your life upon or life around. I'm just on the path. I'm just imagining who I might be, what I might do, for Love and for Kingdom, and trying my damn best to embody that Reality.

Our world is desperate for Saints. It is sold all kinds of lies, all kinds of rituals and routines that lead to emptiness, mediocrity, and the full unmaking of who we are. I walk down the street and I see the languishing, some in rags, and some in pressed suits; I see the loneliness, the insecurity, the suffering. I see the broken hearts, the trembling lips, and

I shake hands with the ill and decrepit. I see the forgotten, on the street corner or alone in a coffee shop; I see the betrayed in the back rows of a church; the abused and the swept aside looking through windows, aching for a shoulder to cry on, arms to fall into. I see the burnout, the exhaustion, the depression. I see the dull eyes, hazy and lifeless, feeling disconnected from any kind of meaning or purpose. I see the hungry and the naked, I see the least of these, the downtrodden and the oppressed, and I see how often our answers are superficial and momentary.

And I see what a Saint would do, could do, in all of those situations. I see heaven meeting earth, offering joy to the languishing, offering compassion and friendship to the lonely, offering real answers to the harsh and brutal and raw questions of life—the ones that aren't sugarcoated or prepackaged, answers that feel less like a definition and more like devotion. I see Saints offering strong shoulders to those with broken hearts. I see Jesus, embodied, through these Saints, offering protection, offering hope, offering rest, offering time and energy and a kind of fullness that echoes with the Life to come. I see that Light reaching into the darkness, and I see the hands of those wandering, lost, confused, reaching out, grasping for us, Saints on the path, not because of what *we* are but because of who we point to.

The Source.

I see an ordinary revolution, a commonplace uprising, an unremarkable overthrow. Ordinary people transformed by an extraordinary God, toppling down sin and Death and darkness and bringing Light and Life and Hope.

I see Every Day Saints transforming the world.

Saints are the Body of Jesus reaching out to the world in Love.

Chapter 39

Selah

MAY CAME TO an end, and so did our time in Spain. The small city of Calpe had transformed from quiet and lonely to loud and riotous. Calpe is a tourist spot, known for its beaches and drunk Brits and Germans burnt red and inebriated before high noon. The sun was hot and our bags and suitcases were packed. We decided to walk from our flat to the bus station to take us to Valencia, one last time through the city.

We walked the winding sidewalk, shops slowly opening, our suitcase wheels bouncing on the interlocking brick. After our time in Europe, it was time to go back, to go home. We were quiet most of the walk, just the rumbling sounds of our suitcases and the humming ebb and flow of a waking city. And our thoughts. It's amazing how much things can change, bit by bit, in such a short time (grand scheme of things, you know?). Taking my mind back to what led us to Europe, who we were, and what our first few days were like, and then comparing to now, it seemed so completely different. My own little metamorphosis. It was the time and space and community to explore a way of living, and that way of living let all of my questions and all of my desires and all of my longings find expression, all of it settling and landing on a freshly tilled internal soil. A seed and soil I could cultivate and watch grow.

We're at the station, and we're sliding our suitcases underneath the bus, in those enormous storage containers, and the driver is scanning our tickets and we climb onto the bus. Our bags go in the overhead compartment and we sit down, holding hands, resting on each other as the drive begins. Serpentine roads through valleys, along the coast, stopping in small seaside towns to pick up people as we go. It's still silent, not many are riding with us, and Aislinn and I are just together. A quiet pause. Time to take a breath and let the reality of transformation wash over us.

There's this idea I learned in Plato, the Greek word for it is *paideia*, and while it's about education, its focus is embodiment. The notion is that by living out the virtues, you teach yourself, from the outside in, about what it means to be Good. It's human transformation by exemplifying a greater Reality. Augustine talked about this, too, in a kind of way, when he discusses *ordo amoris*, or rightly ordered loves. Loving the right stuff the right way in the right priority is the place where all true renewal takes place.

And as we weave the meandering road, I'm just thinking about how, without being taught or told from a pulpit or from a prescribed book, I was given freedom to *embody*. I found, across an ocean, a people with whom I could *live*. It was in the normal comings and goings of life, the fullness of living, the eating and drinking and making merry, the questions and pains and doubts, the hopes and dreams of a future, the disappointments of the past, I learned. And the constant refrain, the chorus that echoed back to me, over pints, on bouldering walls, in walks through parks, seated on a patio overlooking the sea, was one of doing the Good. It was an understanding and an encouraging. A deep Love and appreciation for me, that I existed, that I had my passions and giftings and calling, and then the expectation, the need, for me to use them well. And I felt the same for them, a gratitude for their love, for their giftings, for their personalities and openness, and for how they were in the world. That was the required space to live out this Transcendental Reality and *become*. Or, at least, begin the becoming.

It was a local *paideia*, it was a kind of familial ordering of loves—a unifying under the same Hope. A melody of a new beginning.

It's funny because we expect these things to be some climactic resolution; we're formed on so many narratives that tell us "and then" moments are easy and momentary. That with just a simple bit of movie magic, everything can change. But that wasn't my experience; mine was the slow unfolding path, one step farther every day. It was the light that lit the way through the wilderness and it was the courage to face the slowness of it all.

No instant gratification. It was gradual, the steady and progressive formation, an apprenticeship of the Saints who had gone before me, and those who lived all around me. It was the gentle tuning of my heart, the slow unblocking of my eyes and ears, the calm retraining of my mind, the unhurried disciplining of my body, and then having it all stack and overlap. It was waves of revelation, of being able to feel and see and hear and think and live in the Bright Shadow.

It was first only being able to hear the Hidden Music at a sunset or in a cozy pub, seated by the fireplace. And then it was all around me. It was the blessing of eyes that open in the morning, a chest that rose and fell, fed on the Breath of Life, some dozen or so times every minute. It was the removal of self from the center of my story, taking off the burden of needing to be *something* in order to be someone, and it was a centering vision on Jesus and His Kingdom. It was finding my place in His Grand Story, being blessed and honored to have shared even a moment with Him in His great and loving work of redeeming the cosmos. It was learning to see the Gift of Life, from big to small, to enjoy those Gifts, to perpetuate those Gifts, as all coming from the Source—the Giver.

We get off the bus, we grab our belongings and head into the Valencia airport. It's an easy check-in, and we're seated by our gate in no time at all. The end of an era, it feels like. No one here but us, no one in the airport knowing what had happened, what this all meant. Just people sleeping in seats, leaning on suitcases, hurriedly rushing, and standing in line. Life as normal. No announcement, no badge or ribbon or pat on the back. Just Aislinn leaning her head on my shoulder and the happy smiles of doing what we knew to be Good.

There are very few *big* moments in life. A handful at most, for each of us. Life is not in those big moments. The substance of Life is in the every day, the Holy Ordinary, the common. Life and Love and every Good thing are contained in the normal comings and goings of our days. Our invitation is to join in God's Sacred Sound, His Hidden Music, to which everything, soon, will come into Harmony with. And it is our free choice to reject the invitation, to dance to our own melody, in the hopes it will lead to Life. But it won't. He is the Author of Life, the Source of it—and our every day is either a further up and further in to His Reality, or it is a distancing, a venturing down and a venturing out. That's how I hit Rock Bottom. I was doing Life my way, trying to find salvation in all my addictions and trying to save face with all my lies and cowardice.

And my journey up, my journey into Life, took years.

But now I will never look back.

I'm happy to be ordinary, a man, made and designed for Love. A man created to express Love. An Every Day Saint.

Life is not in the big moments,
life is in the Every Day, the Holy Ordinary.

Chapter 40

There and Back Again

THINGS WERE ALMOST back to normal; we had landed in Toronto, spent some time with family, and then moved into our new place. With roommates. It was a condo near Old Town, the Distillery District, four of us in a two-and-a-half-bedroom unit, one bathroom. Our room looked over the condo's courtyard, our bed pressed up against the window, a desk for Aislinn to teach at, and a closet. A few square feet of open floor.

And then there was rent to deal with; the teaching and design and courier work wasn't going to cover it, so I applied at the bank again and was hired. Back to where it all began. It was novel, at first, coming back "home" after some *grand* adventure, like seeing all the things you loved after a time apart. But the novelty gave way to the hustle and bustle of life, the pace, the noise, the energy.

How could I be a Saint here?

All I knew was that I could try to keep the same sort of embodied vision, the same kind of purposeful living, going. It wasn't the cold hard facts that were going to shape my life, it was the longings fulfilled. It was the reorienting. It was choosing to embrace the invitation of every moment.

I'm up; it's five thirty in the morning, and instead of standing over a double of bourbon, I'm boiling some water and dropping 30 grams of ground coffee into a French press. The condo is dark, and I'm leaning against the counter; the stovetop light is on, and it's quiet, except for the hiss and bubble of water boiling. And there's peace in this silent moment, not the haunting voices in my head, just solitude. The water boils and I pour a half liter over the grinds, and I've got six minutes. I say an *Our Father*, to help frame my coming day. To help me remember that His name is the one to be hallowed, that His will is the one to be done. To remember that my daily bread comes from Him, that forgiveness is a way of Life, and we're always in need of deliverance from our Enemy. The timer goes off, and I pour the steeped coffee into an enamel mug. And the magic isn't lost on me this time. The aromas, the warmth, that beans from Costa Rica have now turned water into java. A miracle.

I've got on gray sweatshorts and a hoodie, and I take my coffee with me out our condo door and over to the elevator. It's silent, save the ding and the opening doors, and I ride down to the basement, where the gym is. *Gym* sounds state-of-the-art; it's just a few machines, a squat rack, and some free weights. I'm sipping at my coffee in between sets, doing a workout, praying and contemplating. Reflecting on some passage while squatting or shoulder pressing or doing pull-ups. This was the same as England, the same as Spain. Sure, it wasn't a bouldering gym, and it wasn't a seaside calisthenics set up; it was in a basement. But it was the same. Time to use my body and time to contemplate. A place to prepare me for the day, to be prepared for all the ways God might invite me to bring heaven to earth.

After my workout, I'm walking back upstairs, coffee mug in hand, and I'm unlocking our unit door, and taking a shower. I grab the clothes I set out the night before, some button-down shirt, chino pants, and put them on. The condo is still quiet, everyone asleep, and I'm packing a lunch, leftovers of beef and rice and broccoli. Then it's the same salute to my sleeping wife, and a prayer for her, and I'm out the door, down the elevator, and waving goodbye to our concierge.

My bike, my trusty steed, is locked up outside, right in front of our building, and my backpack is slung over my shoulders. It's a short ride to the office, some fifteen minutes. The city is still mostly asleep, the trains from out of town haven't yet brought all the workers to their offices. Us cars and cyclists, even the streetcars, we all move to the rhythm of traffic lights, flowing through the city in pre-timed intervals. It's June, so the air on my face and through my hair isn't too cold, and I just breathe it in. Grateful.

I lock up my bike in the back alley behind the office, that same back alley, and there's the same smell in the air, the one I left here some two years ago: vomit and regret. There's people on subway grates to keep warm, there's the empty bottles, there's the trash and the duffel bags. The same stark contrast exists between the main streets, the bright lights, the curated shop windows and the back alley, the broken and battered, the lost and the forgotten. And it's in my mind that this is where a Saint does his work, in the back alley, among the forgotten and the lost, unseen, except by heaven. They're sleeping, so I say a prayer, but I know I'm going to bring them some subs for lunch, and I know I'm going to talk to them, to try to show some Love, the same Love that changed me. I was just like them; I remember the regret on my shoulders, the vomit on my breath, the Death inside. But I heard the Hidden Music. And followed it.

This time the elevator ride up to my floor isn't a bracing or tensing; it's a breath, trying to imagine a *new* way of working, of being a bit of the Life to come in the dreary monotony of a purgatorial nine-to-five. Of wondering what hope and joy looks like, embodied, not just for a day, not just when things are easy, but *always*.

Work is the same as it was before—emails, phone calls, meetings, and Excel spreadsheets; there's the pressure of having everything in your project done faster than possible, the expectation that there's going to be no hiccups or obstacles or upsets, and the wondering what kind of hell will be paid for delays. But I don't feel it quite the same. I see it, and there's the temptation to give in, but that tension in my body, it's telling me something different this time. It's telling me *not* to cope, not to merely survive. It's telling me to search for peace, and then share it. But I don't know how to do that, how to conjure peace, so I just go for a quick walk to a lead designer on my project, and I tell him thanks for all his hard work, thanks for the extra time, and that even though his bosses and the higher-ups might not see it, I appreciate it. And he smiles.

And then, as I'm walking back to my desk, I'm remembering that encouragement is a weapon against hopelessness, that reassurance is a boon against despair. The weapons, not of flesh and blood but the ones that bring in the Kingdom.

Lunchtime comes, and I remember being in line, getting a few ham-and-Swiss subs for those in the back alley. And I'm wondering just how much a sandwich and a few words is really going to do, wondering if it's worth it. And again, I don't really know; but when I think of Jesus and the time He took for the forgotten, I get the impression that maybe I can teach myself compassion by using my body to be generous.

"To stay or to go?" The girl behind the counter is wrapping the subs and either going to put them on a tray or into a bag.

"To go," I say, "and thanks."

She hands me the bag.

Outside, in the back alley, there's a few guys leaned up against the wall, right near my bike. I'm in my pressed chinos and leather boots, my button-down and my slicked-back hair, and they're in whatever they can find. I smell like aftershave and cologne, and they smell like it's been a long time since they've taken care of themselves, like anyone has taken care of them.

"You guys hungry?" I ask.

They look up at me, gaunt, dirty, and a bit suspicious.

"Yeah, man," one of them says.

"I've got a few subs, if you want them," I say as I walk over and squat down beside them, pulling the sandwiches out of the bag. They grab them and start in on eating. I say a prayer, blessing the food and these guys, in my head.

We kind of shoot the breeze, nothing deep, but we talk about the city, and one of them was carving little statues with a knife and some wood blocks. We talk about that for a little while too. And then I check my watch and tell them I've got to get back to it and wish them a good day.

"Thanks, man," they say.

And I tell them, "You're welcome."

The rest of the afternoon is more of the same—emails and phone calls, meetings and spreadsheets. Nothing big, nothing major, nothing to write home about. The hours count down and it's closing in on five, and one of my old work friends comes up, pats me on the shoulder, and asks if I want to go down for drinks.

"Sure," I say. And I know I'm not drinking to survive, not trying to numb the pain or forget; I'm just going to enjoy my time with my friends.

We all meet just before five at the pub, and I tell them first round is on me. And it's not like I could do this every day, I'm thinking, but I could try to learn a bit from my friend from England, the one who showed me that generosity breeds all kinds of joy and gratefulness. And maybe not just for everyone receiving, maybe for the giver too.

They're asking about the trip and my time away, and I'm telling them how amazing it was, but when I share the details, they're all saying it sounded like all I was doing was living normally, the same thing I'd have to do here, just over there.

"That's right," I tell them. "It wasn't a vacation, some great getaway. It was just some time and space to try to figure out how I wanted to spend my life, the normalcy of it all."

"So you worked?" one asks.

"Yeah," I say, "I was doing design stuff and Aislinn was teaching online—she still is. We figured we spend so much time every day doing the same things—grocery shopping, cleaning, cooking, working—that we might as well learn how to do it well."

That's the secret, right? We are what we spend most of our time doing, and most of our time is in the holy, ordinary things, so why not do them well? Why not do them in Love?

Then it's back to other stories and other conversations, and just after six I square up and cycle home. The skies are blue but the horizon is starting to glow red; and the city is alive, thousands moving and pressing, rushing to catch a bus, a train, to get out of the city and go home. Taxis are beeping and pulling off to the side of the road, picking up people waving them down. I'm cycling, the neon lights—some reading "Open," some flashing about food deals or financial loans—are a blur beside me. And I'm thinking that the only way to victory, against dread and bitterness, against the dismay of a hard job, or the day-in-and-day-out routine, is to not be shaped by it. To not let it form you. That was part of what had happened to me. I was formed by my situations because I was passive. Now I had the choice to be active, to choose a way of *being* that endured beyond all the changing circumstances of life. To choose virtue, the way of the Saint, in every small opportunity I got, and to trust that it would keep transforming me.

I get home and because of time zone differences, Aislinn is teaching; I can hear her, in our small room, working through nouns and adjectives and verbs with some students. I get changed quickly, into something a little less corporate, and head out for a walk. I light a cigar, and I'm thinking of all the times I had done this before, and how each of these moments was a time I heard the staggered notes of the Hidden Music. Because I stopped for a moment to listen. My hands are in my pockets, thumbing my lighter and my keys, and I'm leaving a trail of smoke behind me, the smell of vanilla and cedar in the air, and my mind is trying to figure out what I'm experiencing in my body. It's peace, but in a location where once there was chaos. Like walking on water in the midst of a storm.

There is another boardwalk on this side of town, and at the end of it, there is a small beach with lounge chairs, and you could look out over the lake, and *Bluebill* was in the harbor. That's a giant green and white trade ship, a yellow crane moving back and forth on it, "No Smoking" in block letters on the ship's superstructure. The cool of evening has set in, and on the beach there are a few people who have set up a small speaker, and they're playing salsa music and dancing in the sand. I'm leaning back in my chair, smoking, thinking about how life goes on, just the same, day by day. Here, in England, in Spain, everywhere. The lights from the ship and from lampposts are flickering in the water, shimmering on the rippling current. There are people passing by all around me, and I catch parts of their conversations, talking about their days, their plans, their friends, their hopes, their dreams, their pains.

I inhale, the earthy tobacco fills my mouth, and I hold the smoke in and close my eyes, and I'm thinking how so much of our understanding depends on perspective. About how all of Life is about Beholding Jesus so we can see the world His way. The slow exhale, smoke rising, blown away in the wind. Here today, gone tomorrow. But there are things that last, I'm thinking, and there is a way to endure beyond the grave, and all it takes is to commit yourself, fully, to the way of Jesus—farther up and into His Life.

When my cigar is mostly done, I make the walk home, passing under a few bridges, walking through a few alleys, inhaling and exhaling, praying, thinking, reflecting, all at once, that this is the way of an Every Day Saint. It's all any of us can do with a day: our best. To be prayerful, mindful, and follow the path of Virtue.

When I'm home, Ais is done teaching, and she has made us a late dinner. We're sitting at our table, our housemates in their rooms, and we're talking about what it's like to be back. About how it all feels so similar, and how it all feels so different. About how none of us arrive, and there's no vacations on the road to Sainthood.

There are no days off.

Every day counts.

We clean up, telling jokes, laughing, doing the dishes, and wiping the counters, putting everything away, and then we head to the bathroom to wash up, brush our teeth, and then it's off to our room to read or talk before bed. Before we rinse and repeat.

Another day, another opportunity.

And not every day will be like this.

There will still be tons of mistakes, tons of times when I shrug off the invitation to be a Saint, when I give in to anger or apathy, and even drinking. I'm on the same path as you, still learning the hard way. But there has been a *real* change in me. I tasted a bit of the flavor of Death, and I also tasted some of the Life to come, and I know which I prefer.

The Hidden Music is everywhere, if we just have ears to hear.

I had come full circle, but my vision had expanded. And that's the same invitation I now lay before you.

Take a moment to listen, to hear the Hidden Music, and where Jesus might be leading you, all the ways He wants to heal you and transform you, all the ways He wants you to make His Kingdom known; and then, have the courage to take a step. To follow.

It will be hard, the hardest thing you ever do, but it will be an adventure, and it will be Good, and it will lead you Home.

Becoming a Saint does not depend on place, it depends upon perspective and commitment.

A LITURGY OF NEW BEGINNINGS

Formation is not competition, it is offering loaves
 and fish and having God multiply.
Holy Imaginations saturate life with opportunity
 for embodied Sainthood.
Saints are the Body of Jesus reaching out
 to the world in Love.
Life is not in the big moments, life is in
 the Every Day, the Holy Ordinary.
Becoming a Saint does not depend on place,
 it depends upon perspective and commitment.

Find Life; depart the realm of the dead.

Hypocrisy is lethal, hostile to the path of Life.

Learn from those who have walked the Path before,
    they are Guides.

Fear eviscerates the vital organs necessary
    for Sainthood.

Rigorous embodied practice, under tutelage,
    cultivates maturity.

Do not scorn childlike wonder with mere explanation.

Arrogance chokes growth before it can begin.

Desires are signposts that lead to rest.

Souls are reenchanted through the food of Love
    and Wonder.

It is a gift that Life doesn't go as planned.

Souls cannot be restored while bodies
    are neglected.

LITURGY OF THE EVERY DAY SAINT

Faith demands renovation; Grace demolishes that which will not sustain.

Divine Love is not earned, it is a Gift freely given through prayer.

Knowledge alone is insufficient for renewal.

Sainthood is nourished by courage, do not make decisions out of fear.

Grace is sufficient; strength is made perfect in broken places.

God is always speaking, even at the Bottom; have ears to hear.

Only in beholding Jesus is all blindness healed.

In God's Reality there is True Freedom.

Surrender, by listening, to the Way of God.

The full person, body and soul, is an offering; obedience is momentum.

Embodied Love is the path into all Virtue.

Recapture the Beauty of Becoming.

The Ordinary is Holy.

The Every Day composes abiding legacy.

Bodies enact ceremonies which Guide our Loves.

Beauty is the apologetic.

The soul's desire can only be satisfied by the Infinite Jesus.

Virtue, Goodness, is the practice of participating in God's Love.

Jesus is the lens for interpreting the Cosmos; understanding comes by intimacy.

Have eyes to see the Beauty of Jesus in all His Creation.

Embodied Transcendence is the essence of Sainthood.

LITURGY OF THE EVERY DAY SAINT

Bodies teach souls; tune them to the Hidden Music of Jesus.

Bodies are theological, intended to be an Icon of God.

God speaks, most often, in His still small voice; have ears to hear.

Formation is not competition, it is offering loaves and fish and having God multiply.

Holy Imaginations saturate life with opportunity for embodied Sainthood.

Saints are the Body of Jesus reaching out to the world in Love.

Life is not in the big moments, life is in the Every Day, the Holy Ordinary.

Becoming a Saint does not depend on place, it depends upon perspective and commitment.

ACKNOWLEDGMENTS

THE WAY OF the Saint is one of gratitude and continual learning. I have been blessed by the wisdom and care and patience of many along the path, and for that, I am eternally grateful.

Aislinn, you have been with me since the beginning—before this ever became a book, and when we were just living, trying to make our way through the Valley of Shadow. Your love then, when all was unseen, was a Grace that got me through, notes of Hidden Music. And your love now, in all these months of writing, has been the same. A Grace made manifest that got me through. I do not have words. Thank you.

Ben, thank you for inviting me out for beers at The York, for my first-ever British fish-and-chips, for the conversations—the ones that set our hearts on fire, the ones that gave us hope when things seemed dark—and for the prayers. And thanks, even this year, for the Chippie fork for Christmas; it's on my key chain.

Jon, and you, too, Kerry, thanks for the conversations by the fireplace, for pours of nice whiskey, and for answering so many of my questions about ministry, life, and the work of the Spirit. Thanks for answering them with stories, the ones that don't prescribe but the ones that invite. Thanks for taking a few stray Canadians in and feeding them with love every week.

To Lisa-Jo, my editor and sensei, thanks for starting this whole ride—for the messages and emails and conversations. Thanks for reading those early essays and captions, for seeing what it all might become, and thank you for the guidance through the whole writing process.

To Mike, my agent, thanks for the support and encouragement and wisdom, especially in those early days when nothing made sense at all. It was some Michigan love this Canadian needed.

To everyone who was there for me along the way, the pastors who gave support, my friends who sat with me, listened and prayed, those who saw a lost man and opened their homes and hearts, thanks.

I know they'll never read it, but I'm thankful for the pubs I sat and wrote at all those years ago, the boardwalks I trod upon, the courtyard I laid in, looking at the stars. I'm thankful for the subway rides, the basement diners, and the piers. I'm thankful for garden benches and boxing gyms, for all of the places to think and pray.

And to my Lord, I would be gone without You. Thank You for Grace, even at the Bottom. Thank You for Your guiding Spirit, and for the song You have sung over me, the one that led me back to Yourself.

Chapter 1
1. Luke 24:5, CSB

Chapter 3
1. G. K. Chesterton, *The Everlasting Man*, 5th ed. (Hodder and Stoughton, 1954), 116–7.

Chapter 4
1. Thomas R. Whissen, *The Devil's Advocates: Decadence in Modern Literature* (Bloomsbury Academic, 1989), 69.
2. C. S. Lewis, *The Abolition of Man* (HarperCollins, 2001), e-book 26.

Chapter 6
1. G. K. Chesterton, *Tremendous Trifles*, originally published 1909, republished by Project Gutenberg, 2003, https://www.gutenberg.org/files/8092/8092-h/8092-h.htm.
2. G. K. Chesterton, *Orthodoxy* (The Bodley Head, 1909), 174.
3. C. S. Lewis, *An Experiment in Criticism* (Faded Page, 1961), e-book, 69.
4. Luke 24:5, CSB

Chapter 7
1. Fyodor Dostoevsky, *Notes from Underground* and *The Double* (Penguin Classics, 1972), 32.

Chapter 8
1. John Steinbeck, *The Winter of Our Discontent* (Penguin, 2008), 101.
2. St. Augustine, *Confessions and Enchiridion*, trans. Albert C. Outler (Christian Classics Ethereal Library, 1955), bk. 2, 37, https://www.ccel.org/ccel/augustine/confessions.html.
3. St. Augustine, *Confessions and Enchiridion*, bk. 1, 13.

Chapter 9
1. C. S. Lewis, *The Magician's Nephew* (HarperCollins, 1994), 92, e-book.
2. Thomas Moore, *The Re-Enchantment of Everyday Life* (HarperCollins, 1996), ix.

Chapter 11
1. G. K. Chesterton, *St. Thomas Aquinas: The Dumb Ox* (Angelico Press, 1974), 14.
2. Pope John Paul II, *Man and Woman He Created Them*: A Theology of the Body (Pauline Books and Media, 2006), 203.

Chapter 12
1. Proverbs 26:11
2. Bob Dylan, "Shelter from the Storm," recorded on September 17, 1974, track 9 on *Blood on the Tracks,* Columbia Records, 1975, 33⅓ rpm.
3. Ecclesiastes 1:2–3 (emphasis mine)
4. Ecclesiastes 1:5, 7 (emphasis mine)
5. Ecclesiastes 2:11 (emphasis mine)
6. C. S. Lewis, *A Grief Observed* (HarperSanFrancisco, 2001), 52.

Chapter 13
1. Matthew 22:37

Chapter 14
1. James 2:19

Chapter 15
1. Georg W. F. Hegel, *Elements of the Philosophy of Right* (Cambridge University Press, 1991), 23.

Chapter 16
1. Fyodor Dostoevsky, *The Brothers Karamazov*, trans. Richard Pevear and Larissa Volokhonsky (Knopf, 1992), 58.
2. Oscar Wilde, *De Profundis: The Ballad of Reading Gaol and Other Writings* (Wordsworth Classics, 2002), 73.
3. Ernest Hemingway, *A Farewell to Arms* (Scribner Classic, 1997), 130.

Chapter 18
1. St. Augustine, *Confessions*, trans. Albert C. Outler, originally published 1955, https://www.ling.upenn.edu/courses/hum100/augustinconf.pdf, 126.
2. 1 Corinthians 13:12, KJV
3. Julian of Norwich, *Revelations of Divine Love* (Wilder Publications, 2011), 94.
4. Gregory of Nyssa, *The Life of Moses* (Paulist Press, 1978), 115.

Chapter 19
1. C. S. Lewis, *The Collected Letters of C. S. Lewis*, vol. 3, ed. Walter Hooper (HarperCollins, 2009), 465, e-book.

2. G. K. Chesterton, *Orthodoxy* (The Bodley Head, 1909), 174.
3. Albert Camus, *The Plague*, trans. Stuart Gilbert, first published 1948, https://ratical.org/PandemicParallaxView/ThePlague-Camus.pdf, 62.
4. Camus, *The Plague*, 137.

Chapter 21

1. Friedrich Nietzsche, *Beyond Good and Evil*, trans. Helen Zimmern (rep. by Project Gutenburg, 2009), https://www.gutenberg.org/files/4363/4363-h/4363-h.htm.
2. John 12:24–26
3. Matthew 12:43–45

Chapter 22

1. It should be noted, the popular usage of this quote seems to tweak the original from Clement of Rome, *First Epistle of Clement to the Corinthians*, trans. J. B. Lightfoot, 1990, Athena Data Products, https://www.ntslibrary.com/PDF%20Books/First%20Epistle%20of%20Clement%20to%20the%20Corinthians.pdf.
2. 1 Corinthians 12:31–13:13 (emphasis mine)
3. James K. Smith, *You Are What You Love: The Spiritual Power of Habit* (Brazos Press, 2014), 19.

Chapter 23

1. This quote is often falsely attributed to C. S. Lewis. Original source unknown.
2. This quote was likely derived from a passage written by Antoine de Saint-Exupéry in *Citadelle*. See "Teach Them to Yearn for the Vast and Endless Sea," Quote Investigator, August 25, 2015, https://quoteinvestigator.com/2015/08/25/sea/.

Chapter 25

1. John Steinbeck, *East of Eden* (Penguin, 2002), 213.
2. Soetsu Yanagi, *The Beauty of Everyday Things*, trans. Michael Brase (Penguin Random House, 2017), 8–9.

Chapter 26

1. John Paul II, *Theology of the Body in Simple Language*, adap. by Philokalia Books (CreateSpace Independent Publishing, 2008), 8.
2. Matthew 10:39

Chapter 27

1. G. K. Chesterton, *Orthodoxy* (The Bodley Head, 1909), 13.
2. Chesterton, *Orthodoxy*, 16–17.

3. C. S. Lewis, *The Weight of Glory* (HarperOne, 1980), 42–3.
4. Matthew 22:36–40 (emphasis mine)

Chapter 28
1. Henri Nouwen, *The Return of the Prodigal Son: Anniversary Edition* (Crown, 2016), 123.
2. C. S. Lewis, *Mere Christianity* (HarperCollins, 2001), 136–7, e-book.
3. Peter Kreeft, "The Argument From Desire," excerpted from Peter Kreeft, Ronald K. Tacelli, *The Handbook of Christian Apologetics* (IVP Academic, 1994), accessed December 5, 2023, https://www.peterkreeft.com/topics/desire.htm.

Chapter 29
1. This is a riff on a quote from G. K. Chesterton, *The Everlasting Man*, 5th ed. (Hodder and Stoughton, 1954), 198.
2. Ridley Scott, dir., *Gladiator* (United States: DreamWorks Pictures, 2000).
3. C. S. Lewis, *The Screwtape Letters* (Collins Fount Paperbacks, 1980), 148.

Chapter 30
1. This is, in fact, a very deep philosophical and theological idea: the essence-energy distinction. God is unknowable in His essence, so we can only understand Him by his energies—His workings and actions.
2. John 1:14
3. John 14:9

Chapter 31
1. G. K. Chesterton, *Orthodoxy* (The Bodley Head, 1909), 94.
2. C. S. Lewis, *Surprised by Joy: The Shape of My Early Life* (Harcourt, Brace, Jovanovich, 1996), 181.

Chapter 34
1. James K. Smith, *You Are What You Love: The Spiritual Power of Habit* (Brazos Press, 2014).
2. Peter Gentry and Stephen Wellum, *Kingdom Through Covenant: A Biblical-Theological Understanding of the Covenants* (Crossway, 2012), 192–94.
3. Pope John Paul II, *Man and Woman He Created Them: A Theology of the Body* (Pauline Books and Media, 2006), 154.
4. Pope John Paul II, *Man and Woman He Created Them*, 183.
5. G. K. Chesterton, *St. Thomas Aquinas: The Dumb Ox* (Angelico Press, 1974), 14.

Chapter 35
1. Stephen Turley, *Awakening Wonder: A Classical Guide to Truth, Goodness & Beauty* (Classical Academic Press, 2015), Kindle edition 37.

2. Maximos the Confessor, *On the Cosmic Mystery of Jesus Christ*, trans. Paul M. Blowers and Robert L. Wilkin (St. Vladimir's Seminary Press, 2003), 70.
3. Athanasius of Alexandria, *On the Incarnation*, trans. Penelope Lawson, (St. Vladimir's Seminary Press, 2016), e-book 14.
4. Oscar Wilde, *The Picture of Dorian Gray* (Oxford University Press, 2006), 21.

Chapter 36
1. Matthew 23:26

Chapter 37
1. C. S. Lewis, *Selected Literary Essays* (HarperOne, 2013), 146, e-book.
2. Lewis, *Selected Literary Essays*, 146.
3. Lewis, 147.
4. Lewis, 147.
5. Wendell Berry, *Conversations with Wendell Berry*, ed. Morris A. Grubbs, (University Press of Mississippi, 2007), 177.
6. This is a well-known paraphrase of a quote by G. K. Chesterton from the chapter "The Red Angel" in his work *Tremendous Trifles*.
7. Chuck Palahniuk, *Choke: A Novel* (Anchor Books, 2002), e-book loc. 2096.

ABOUT THE AUTHOR

JOSH NADEAU IS AN ARTIST and author from West Coast Canada. His work seeks to translate ancient ideas of embodying the Reality of God for a modern time. Beauty is the apologetic for inviting others to reimagine the holy ordinary of every day life as part of God's Transcendent Work.

He has appeared on numerous podcasts, written articles for magazines and websites, and has created art for Jordan Peterson's History of Western Civilization, as well as churches, musicians, and organizations like the Chosen, Searock, Bless God, and more.

He is husband to Aislinn, father to Ransom, and spends his days reading, writing, bouldering, and trying to enjoy every good and perfect gift. He has his undergraduate degree in physics, a master's in theological studies, and a doctorate from the school of hard knocks.

Josh is the founder of Sword and Pencil and Every Day Saints.